awesome WORDS

awesome
WORDS

DAILY BIBLE READINGS FOR TEENS

COMPILED BY
EDYTHE ANNE DRAPER

CROSSWAY BOOKS
WHEATON, ILLINOIS

Awesome Words

Copyright © 2008 by Edythe Anne Draper

Published by Crossway Books
a publishing ministry of Good News Publishers
1300 Crescent Street
Wheaton, Illinois 60187

Cover design: Amy Bristow

Cover illustration and all interior illustrations: iStock

First printing 2008

Printed in the United States of America

USING THIS BOOK: Words in italics have been changed from the English Standard Version in order to make the verses quoted fit together more consistently in terms of plural and singular pronouns and verbs. However, the opening verse in each day's entry is in bold capital letters. Words in brackets have been changed or supplied when needed to tell the reader to whom or what the verse refers. Scripture used is from the Single Column Reference Edition of the English Standard Version, copyright 2007.

PDF ISBN: 978-1-4335-0421-9

Mobipocket ISBN: 978-1-4335-0422-7

Library of Congress Cataloging-in-Publication Data
Bible. English. English Standard. Selections. 2008.
  Awesome words : daily Bible readings for teens / compiled by Edythe Anne Draper.
    p. cm.
  ISBN 978-1-58134-953-5 (tpb)
  1. Bible—Quotations. 2. Devotional calendars. 3. Teenagers—Religious life. I. Draper, Edythe. II. Title.
BS416.B49   2008
220.5'208—dc22   2008000509

DP		17	16	15	14	13	12	11		10	09	08
15	14	13	12	11	10	9	8	7	6	5	4	3	2	1

THE PRECEPTS OF THE LORD ARE RIGHT,
rejoicing the heart; the commandment of the Lord is pure, enlightening the eyes.

Length of days and years of life and peace they will add to you. Let not steadfast love and faithfulness forsake you; bind them around your neck; write them on the tablet of your heart. So you will find favor and good success in the sight of God and man.

Trust in the Lord with all your heart, and do not lean on your own understanding. In all your ways acknowledge him, and he will make straight your paths.

Psalm 19:8 Proverbs 3:2-6

APPLY YOUR HEART TO INSTRUCTION AND YOUR EAR TO WORDS OF KNOWLEDGE.

No eye has seen, nor ear heard, nor the heart of man imagined, what God has prepared for those who love him.

For the eyes of the LORD run to and fro throughout the whole earth, to give strong support to those whose heart is blameless toward him.

Let no one despise you for your youth, but set the believers an example in speech, in conduct, in love, in faith, in purity.

Delight yourself in the LORD, and he will give you the desires of your heart.

Proverbs 23:12. 1 Corinthians 2:9. 2 Chronicles 16:9. 1 Timothy 4:12. Psalm 37:4.

WALK IN A MANNER WORTHY OF THE LORD, FULLY PLEASING TO HIM, BEARING FRUIT IN EVERY GOOD WORK AND INCREASING IN THE KNOWLEDGE OF GOD.

The LORD gives wisdom; from his mouth come knowledge and understanding; he stores up sound wisdom for the upright; he is a shield to those who walk in integrity, guarding the paths of justice and watching over the way of his saints.

Then you will understand righteousness and justice and equity, every good path; for wisdom will come into your heart, and knowledge will be pleasant to your soul; discretion will watch over you, understanding will guard you.

Colossians 1:10. Proverbs 2:6-11.

LOOKING TO JESUS, THE FOUNDER AND PERFECTER OF MY FAITH.

I lift up my eyes to the hills. From where does my help come? My help comes from the LORD, who made heaven and earth.

He will not let *my* foot be moved; he who keeps *me* will not slumber. Behold, he who keeps Israel will neither slumber nor sleep.

The LORD is *my* keeper; the LORD is *my* shade on *my* right hand. The sun shall not strike *me* by day, nor the moon by night.

The LORD will keep *me* from all evil; he will keep *my* life. The LORD will keep *my* going out and *my* coming in from this time forth and forevermore.

The Lord will rescue me from every evil deed and bring me safely into his heavenly kingdom. To him be the glory forever and ever. Amen.

Hebrews 12:2. Psalm 121:1-8. 2 Timothy 4:18.

PUT ON THE ARMOR OF LIGHT.

Walk properly as in the daytime. . . . Put on the Lord Jesus Christ, and make no provision for the flesh, to gratify its desires.

For you are all children of light, children of the day. *You* are not of the night or of the darkness.

Do all things without grumbling or questioning, that you may be blameless and innocent, children of God without blemish in the midst of a crooked and twisted generation, among whom you shine as lights in the world.

The LORD God is a sun and shield; the LORD bestows favor and honor. No good thing does he withhold from those who walk uprightly.

Romans 13:12-14. 1 Thessalonians 5:5. Philippians 2:14-15. Psalm 84:11.

BE IMITATORS OF GOD,
AS BELOVED CHILDREN.

Walk in love, as Christ loved *you* and gave himself up for *you*, a fragrant offering and sacrifice to God.

Let there be no filthiness nor foolish talk nor crude joking, which are out of place, but instead let there be thanksgiving.

At one time you were darkness, but now you are light in the Lord. Walk as children of light (for the fruit of light is found in all that is good and right and true), and try to discern what is pleasing to the Lord.

Ephesians 5:1-2, 4, 8-10.

AS YOU RECEIVED CHRIST JESUS THE LORD,
SO WALK IN HIM—

rooted and built up in him and established in the faith, just as you were taught, abounding in thanksgiving.

See to it that no one takes you captive by philosophy and empty deceit, according to human tradition, according to the elemental spirits of the world, and not according to Christ.

Set your minds on things that are above, not on things that are on earth.

Put on then, as God's chosen ones, holy and beloved, compassionate hearts, kindness, humility, meekness, and patience, bearing with one another and, if one has a complaint against another, forgiving each other; as the Lord has forgiven you, so you also must forgive. And above all these put on love, which binds everything together in perfect harmony.

Colossians 2:6-8. Colossians 3:2, 12-14.

LET ALL BITTERNESS AND WRATH AND ANGER AND CLAMOR AND SLANDER BE PUT AWAY FROM YOU, ALONG WITH ALL MALICE.

Therefore, having put away falsehood, let each one of you speak the truth with his neighbor, for we are members one of another. Be angry and do not sin; do not let the sun go down on your anger, and give no opportunity to the devil. Let the thief no longer steal, but rather let him labor, doing honest work with his own hands, so that he may have something to share with anyone in need.

Let no corrupting talk come out of your mouths, but only such as is good for building up, as fits the occasion, that it may give grace to those who hear.

Be kind to one another, tenderhearted, forgiving one another, as God in Christ forgave you.

Ephesians 4:31. Ephesians 4:25-28, 29, 32.

FAITH, HOPE, AND LOVE ABIDE, THESE THREE; BUT THE GREATEST OF THESE IS LOVE.

Love is patient and kind; love does not envy or boast; it is not arrogant or rude. It does not insist on its own way; it is not irritable or resentful; it does not rejoice at wrongdoing, but rejoices with the truth. Love bears all things, believes all things, hopes all things, endures all things. Love never ends. As for prophecies, they will pass away; as for tongues, they will cease; as for knowledge, it will pass away. For we know in part and we prophesy in part, but when the perfect comes, the partial will pass away.

For now we see in a mirror dimly, but then face to face. Now *we* know in part; then *we* shall know fully.

Love one another earnestly from a pure heart.

1 Corinthians 13:13. 1 Corinthians 13:4-10, 12. 1 Peter 1:22.

LOVE COVERS A MULTITUDE OF SINS.

Jesus said . . . , "A new commandment I give to you, that you love one another: just as I have loved you, you also are to love one another."

Do not repay evil for evil or reviling for reviling, but on the contrary, bless, for to this you were called, that you may obtain a blessing.

Hatred stirs up strife, but love covers all offenses.

Let us not love in word or talk but in deed and in truth.

I am writing these things to you so that you may not sin. But if anyone does sin, we have an advocate with the Father, Jesus Christ the righteous. He is the propitiation for our sins, and not for ours only but also for the sins of the whole world. And by this we know that we have come to know him, if we keep his commandments.

1 Peter 4:8. John 13:31, 34. 1 Peter 3:9. Proverbs 10:12. 1 John 3:18. 1 John 2:1-3.

PUT FALSE WAYS FAR FROM ME AND GRACIOUSLY TEACH ME YOUR LAW!

I have chosen the way of faithfulness; I set your rules before me. I cling to your testimonies, O LORD; let me not be put to shame! I will run in the way of your commandments when you enlarge my heart!

Teach me, O LORD, the way of your statutes; and I will keep it to the end. Give me understanding, that I may keep your law and observe it with my whole heart. Lead me in the path of your commandments, for I delight in it.

Incline my heart to your testimonies, and not to selfish gain! Turn my eyes from looking at worthless things; and give me life in your ways.

Psalm 119:29-37.

EVERYONE WHO CALLS ON THE NAME OF
THE LORD SHALL BE SAVED.

If you confess with your mouth that Jesus is Lord and believe in your heart that God raised him from the dead, you will be saved. For with the heart one believes and is justified, and with the mouth one confesses and is saved.

If anyone is in Christ, he is a new creation. The old has passed away; behold, the new has come.

Then you will understand righteousness and justice and equity, every good path; for wisdom will come into your heart, and knowledge will be pleasant to your soul.

Joel 2:32. Romans 10:9-10. 2 Corinthians 5:17. Proverbs 2:9-10.

CALLED TO BELONG TO JESUS CHRIST.

The LORD has set apart the godly for himself.

He will deliver you from the snare of the fowler and from the deadly pestilence. He will cover you with his pinions, and under his wings you will find refuge; his faithfulness is a shield and buckler. You will not fear the terror of the night, nor the arrow that flies by day, nor the pestilence that stalks in darkness, nor the destruction that wastes at noonday.

For he will command his angels concerning you to guard you in all your ways.

Romans 1:6. Psalm 4:3. Psalm 91:3-6, 11.

THE LORD IS AT HAND.

According to his promise we are waiting for new heavens and a new earth in which righteousness dwells.

For the Lord himself will descend from heaven with a cry of command, with the voice of an archangel, and with the sound of the trumpet of God. And the dead in Christ will rise first. Then we who are alive, who are left, will be caught up together with them in the clouds to meet the Lord in the air, and so we will always be with the Lord.

Therefore, beloved, since you are waiting for these, be diligent to be found by him without spot or blemish, and at peace.

Philippians 4:5. 2 Peter 3:13. 1 Thessalonians 4:16-17. 2 Peter 3:14.

WHILE THE EARTH REMAINS, SEEDTIME AND HARVEST, COLD AND HEAT, SUMMER AND WINTER, DAY AND NIGHT, SHALL NOT CEASE.

The earth is the LORD's and the fullness thereof, the world and those who dwell therein, for he has founded it upon the seas and established it upon the rivers.

Sing to the Lord with thanksgiving; make melody to our God on the lyre!

He gives snow like wool; he scatters hoarfrost like ashes. He hurls down his crystals of ice like crumbs; who can stand before his cold? He sends out his word, and melts them; he makes his wind blow and the waters flow.

He covers the heavens with clouds; he prepares rain for the earth; he makes grass grow on the hills. He gives to the beasts their food, and to the young ravens that cry.

He makes peace in your borders; he fills you with the finest of the wheat.

Genesis 8:22. Psalm 24:1-2. Psalm 147:7, 16-18. Psalm 147:8-9, 14.

BLESS THE LORD, O MY SOUL!

O LORD my God, you are very great! You are clothed with splendor and majesty, covering yourself with light as with a garment, stretching out the heavens like a tent.

You lay the beams of *your* chambers on the waters; *you make* the clouds *your* chariot; *you ride* on the wings of the wind; *you make your* messengers winds, *your* ministers a flaming fire.

You set the earth on its foundations, so that it should never be moved. You covered it with the deep as with a garment; the waters stood above the mountains. At your rebuke they fled; at the sound of your thunder they took to flight. You set a boundary that they may not pass, so that they might not again cover the earth.

The mountains rose, the valleys sank down to the place that you appointed for them.

Psalm 104:1-7, 9. Psalm 104:8.

> "Sing to the Lord with thanksgiving; make melody to our God on the lyre!"

O LORD, HOW MANIFOLD ARE YOUR WORKS!
IN WISDOM HAVE YOU MADE THEM ALL;
THE EARTH IS FULL OF YOUR CREATURES.

You make springs gush forth in the valleys; they flow between the hills; they give drink to every beast of the field; the wild donkeys quench their thirst. Beside them the birds of the heavens dwell; they sing among the branches. From your lofty abode you water the mountains; the earth is satisfied with the fruit of your work.

You cause the grass to grow for the livestock and plants *to grow* for man to cultivate, that he may bring forth food from the earth and wine to gladden the heart of man, oil to make his face shine and bread to strengthen man's heart.

The trees of the LORD are watered abundantly, the cedars of Lebanon that he planted. In them the birds build their nests; the stork has her home in the fir trees. The high mountains are for the wild goats; the rocks are a refuge for the rock badgers.

Psalm 104:24. Psalm 104:10-18.

SEEK THE LORD AND LIVE.

He who made the Pleiades and Orion, and turns deep darkness into the morning and darkens the day into night, who calls for the waters of the sea and pours them out on the surface of the earth, the LORD is his name.

Who has ascended to heaven and come down? Who has gathered the wind in his fists? Who has wrapped up the waters in a garment? Who has established all the ends of the earth? What is his name, and what is his son's name? Surely you know!

Know the God of your father and serve him with a whole heart and with a willing mind, for the LORD searches all hearts and understands every plan and thought. If you seek him, he will be found by you.

Amos 5:6, 8. Proverbs 30:4. 1 Chronicles 28:9.

BE SURE YOUR SIN WILL FIND YOU OUT.

If we say we have fellowship with him while we walk in darkness, we lie and do not practice the truth. But if we walk in the light, as he is in the light, we have fellowship with one another, and the blood of Jesus his Son cleanses us from all sin.

If we say we have no sin, we deceive ourselves, and the truth is not in us. If we confess our sins, he is faithful and just to forgive us our sins and to cleanse us from all unrighteousness.

Purge me with hyssop, and I shall be clean; wash me, and I shall be whiter than snow. Let me hear joy and gladness; let the bones that you have broken rejoice. Hide your face from my sins, and blot out all my iniquities.

Create in me a clean heart, O God, and renew a right spirit within me. Cast me not away from your presence, and take not your Holy Spirit from me. Restore to me the joy of your salvation, and uphold me with a willing spirit.

Numbers 32:23. 1 John 1:6-9. Psalm 51:7-12.

WHAT IS LACKING IN YOUR FAITH?

Now in a great house there are not only vessels of gold and silver but also of wood and clay, some for honorable use, some for dishonorable. Therefore, if anyone cleanses himself from what is dishonorable, he will be a vessel for honorable use, set apart as holy, useful to the master of the house, ready for every good work.

So flee youthful passions and pursue righteousness, faith, love, and peace, along with those who call on the Lord from a pure heart. Have nothing to do with foolish, ignorant controversies; you know that they breed quarrels.

May the Lord make you increase and abound in love for one another . . . so that he may establish your hearts blameless in holiness before our God and Father, at the coming of our Lord Jesus with all his saints.

1 Thessalonians 3:10. 2 Timothy 2:20-23. 1 Thessalonians 3:12-13.

EVERYONE WHO ACKNOWLEDGES ME [JESUS] BEFORE MEN, I ALSO WILL ACKNOWLEDGE BEFORE MY FATHER WHO IS IN HEAVEN.

Nevertheless, many even of the authorities believed in him, but for fear of the Pharisees they did not confess it, so that they would not be put out of the synagogue; for they loved the glory that comes from man more than the glory that comes from God.

God gave us a spirit not of fear but of power and love and self-control. Therefore do not be ashamed of the testimony about our Lord . . . who saved us and called us to a holy calling, not because of our works but because of his own purpose and grace, which he gave us in Christ Jesus before the ages began.

If you are insulted for the name of Christ, you are blessed, because the Spirit of glory and of God rests upon you.

Matthew 10:32. John 12:42-43. 2 Timothy 1:7-9. 1 Peter 4:14.

JESUS SAID . . . "I AM THE WAY, AND THE TRUTH, AND THE LIFE."

The Spirit of the Lord GOD is upon me, because the LORD has anointed me to bring good news to the poor; he has sent me to bind up the brokenhearted, to proclaim liberty to the captives, and the opening of the prison to those who are bound; to proclaim the year of the LORD's favor, and the day of vengeance of our God; to comfort all who mourn.

Jesus is the Christ . . . the Alpha and the Omega, the first and the last, the beginning and the end.

John 14:6. Isaiah 61:1-2. 1 John 5:1. Revelation 22:13.

WHOEVER KEEPS HIS WORD, IN HIM TRULY
THE LOVE OF GOD IS PERFECTED.

By this we may be sure that we are in him: whoever says he abides in him ought to walk in the same way in which he walked.

And by this we know that we have come to know him, if we keep his commandments. Whoever says "I know him" but does not keep his commandments is a liar, and the truth is not in him.

No one born of God makes a practice of sinning, for God's seed abides in him, and he cannot keep on sinning because he has been born of God. By this it is evident who are the children of God, and who are the children of the devil: whoever does not practice righteousness is not of God, nor is the one who does not love his brother.

1 John 2:5-6. 1 John 2:3-4. 1 John 3:9-10.

AS YOU WISH THAT OTHERS WOULD DO TO YOU,
DO SO TO THEM.

If you love those who love you, what benefit is that to you? For even sinners love those who love them.

And if you do good to those who do good to you, what benefit is that to you? For even sinners do the same.

And if you lend to those from whom you expect to receive, what credit is that to you? Even sinners lend to sinners, to get back the same amount.

But love your enemies, and do good, and lend, expecting nothing in return, and your reward will be great, and you will be sons of the Most High, for he is kind to the ungrateful and the evil.

Luke 6:31-35.

THE HEARING EAR AND THE SEEING EYE, THE LORD HAS MADE THEM BOTH.

God said, "Let us make man in our image, after our likeness. And let them have dominion over the fish of the sea and over the birds of the heavens and over the livestock and over all the earth and over every creeping thing that creeps on the earth."

You *[God]* formed my inward parts; you knitted me together in my mother's womb. I praise you, for I am fearfully and wonderfully made. Wonderful are your works; my soul knows it very well.

Your eyes saw my unformed substance; in your book were written, every one of them, the days that were formed for me, when as yet there was none of them.

Both riches and honor come from you, and you rule over all. In your hand are power and might, and in your hand it is to make great and to give strength to all. And now we thank you, our God, and praise your glorious name.

Proverbs 20:12. Genesis 1:26. Psalm 139:13-14, 16. 1 Chronicles 29:12-13.

KEEP YOUR TONGUE FROM EVIL AND YOUR LIPS FROM SPEAKING DECEIT.

A man who bears false witness against his neighbor is like a war club, or a sword, or a sharp arrow. Trusting in a treacherous man in time of trouble is like a bad tooth or a foot that slips.

Whoever desires to love life and see good days, let him keep his tongue from evil and his lips from speaking deceit; let him turn away from evil and do good; let him seek peace and pursue it. For the eyes of the Lord are on the righteous, and his ears are open to their prayer. But the face of the Lord is against those who do evil.

Psalm 34:13. Proverbs 25:18-19. 1 Peter 3:10-12.

EVIL PEOPLE AND IMPOSTORS WILL GO ON FROM BAD TO WORSE, DECEIVING AND BEING DECEIVED.

But as for you, continue in what you have learned and have firmly believed, knowing from whom you learned it.

Beware of false prophets, who come to you in sheep's clothing but inwardly are ravenous wolves. You will recognize them by their fruits. Are grapes gathered from thorn bushes, or figs from thistles?

Not everyone who says to me, "Lord, Lord," will enter the kingdom of heaven, but the one who does the will of my Father who is in heaven.

2 Timothy 3:13-14. Matthew 7:15-16, 21.

[O LORD,] TURN MY EYES FROM LOOKING AT WORTHLESS THINGS; AND GIVE ME LIFE IN YOUR WAYS.

His divine power has granted to us all things that pertain to life and godliness, through the knowledge of him who called us to his own glory and excellence. . . . He has granted to us his precious and very great promises, so that through them you may become partakers of the divine nature.

For this very reason, make every effort to supplement your faith with virtue . . .

knowledge . . .

self-control . . .

steadfastness . . .

godliness . . .

brotherly affection . . .

love.

For if these qualities are yours and are increasing, they keep you from being ineffective or unfruitful in the knowledge of our Lord Jesus Christ.

Psalm 119:37. 2 Peter 1:3-8.

I HAVE THE DESIRE TO DO WHAT IS RIGHT,
BUT NOT THE ABILITY TO CARRY IT OUT.

I do not understand my own actions. For I do not do what I want, but I do the very thing I hate.

The LORD looks down from heaven on the children of man, to see if there are any who understand, who seek after God. They have all turned aside; together they have become corrupt; there is none who does good, not even one.

The steadfast love of the LORD never ceases; his mercies never come to an end; they are new every morning; great is *his* faithfulness. Let us test and examine our ways, and return to the LORD! The LORD is good to those who wait for him, to the soul who seeks him.

Romans 7:18. Romans 7:15. Psalm 14:2-3. Lamentations 3:22-23, 40. Lamentations 3:25.

THE APOSTLES RETURNED TO JESUS AND TOLD HIM
ALL THAT THEY HAD DONE AND TAUGHT.

Do not be anxious about anything, but in everything by prayer and supplication with thanksgiving let your requests be made known to God. And the peace of God, which surpasses all understanding, will guard your hearts and your minds in Christ Jesus.

You did not receive the spirit of slavery to fall back into fear, but you have received the Spirit of adoption as sons, by whom we cry, "Abba! Father!"

So you are no longer a slave, but a son, and if a son, then an heir through God.

Let us then with confidence draw near to the throne of grace, that we may receive mercy and find grace to help in time of need.

Mark 6:30. Philippians 4:6-7. Romans 8:15. Galatians 4:7. Hebrews 4:16.

THE WORD OF GOD IS LIVING AND ACTIVE—

—sharper than any two-edged sword, piercing to the division of soul and of spirit, of joints and of marrow, and discerning the thoughts and intentions of the heart. And no creature is hidden from *God's* sight, but all are naked and exposed to the eyes of him to whom we must give account.

My little children, I am writing these things to you so that you may not sin. But if anyone does sin, we have an advocate with the Father, Jesus Christ the righteous. He is the propitiation for our sins, and not for ours only but also for the sins of the whole world.

Hebrews 4:12-13. 1 John 2:1-2.

LISTEN TO ADVICE AND ACCEPT INSTRUCTION, THAT YOU MAY GAIN WISDOM IN THE FUTURE.

God gave Solomon wisdom and understanding beyond measure, and breadth of mind like the sand on the seashore, so that Solomon's wisdom surpassed the wisdom of all the people of the east and all the wisdom of Egypt.

Behold, the fear of the Lord, that is wisdom, and to turn away from evil is understanding.

Everyone then who hears these words of mine and does them will be like a wise man who built his house on the rock. And the rain fell, and the floods came, and the winds blew and beat on that house, but it did not fall, because it had been founded on the rock.

He who fathers a wise son will be glad in him. Let your father and mother be glad.

Proverbs 19:20. 1 Kings 4:29-30. Job 28:28. Matthew 7:24-25. Proverbs 23:24-25.

EVERY WAY OF A MAN IS RIGHT IN HIS OWN EYES, BUT THE LORD WEIGHS THE HEART.

The LORD knows the way of the righteous, but the way of the wicked will perish.

The LORD will show who is his, and who is holy. The Helper, the Holy Spirit . . . will teach you all things.

O great and mighty God, whose name is the LORD of hosts, great in counsel and mighty in deed, whose eyes are open to all the ways of the children of man, rewarding each one according to his ways and according to the fruit of his deeds. Search me, O God, and know my heart! Try me and know my thoughts! And see if there be any grievous way in me, and lead me in the way everlasting!

Proverbs 21:2. Psalm 1:6. Numbers 16:5. John 14:26. Jeremiah 32:18-19. Psalm 139:23-24.

LET YOUR ADORNING BE THE HIDDEN PERSON OF THE HEART WITH THE IMPERISHABLE BEAUTY OF A GENTLE AND QUIET SPIRIT, WHICH IN GOD'S SIGHT IS VERY PRECIOUS.

Agree with one another, live in peace. Whoever is slow to anger is better than the mighty, and he who rules his spirit than he who takes a city.

A soft answer turns away wrath, but a harsh word stirs up anger. A hot-tempered man stirs up strife, but he who is slow to anger quiets contention. Have nothing to do with irreverent, silly myths. Rather train yourself for godliness; for while bodily training is of some value, godliness is of value in every way.

For the grace of God has appeared, bringing salvation for all people, training us to renounce ungodliness and worldly passions, and to live self-controlled, upright, and godly lives. Pursue righteousness, godliness, faith, love, steadfastness, gentleness.

1 Peter 3:4. 2 Corinthians 13:11. Proverbs 16:32. Proverbs 15:1, 18. 1 Timothy 4:7-8. Titus 2:11-12. 1 Timothy 6:11.

SEE WHAT KIND OF LOVE THE FATHER HAS GIVEN TO US, THAT WE SHOULD BE CALLED CHILDREN OF GOD; AND SO WE ARE.

The Spirit himself bears witness with our spirit that we are children of God, and if children, then heirs—heirs of God and fellow heirs with Christ. . . .

God gave us eternal life, and this life is in his Son. Whoever has the Son has life; whoever does not have the Son of God does not have life. I write these things to you who believe in the name of the Son of God that you may know that you have eternal life. And we know that the Son of God has come and has given us understanding, so that we may know him who is true. . . . He is the true God and eternal life.

There will be richly provided for you an entrance into the eternal kingdom of our Lord and Savior Jesus Christ.

1 John 3:1. Romans 8:16-17. 1 John 5:11-13, 20. 2 Peter 1:11.

O LORD, YOU HAVE SEARCHED ME AND KNOWN ME!

You know when I sit down and when I rise up; you discern my thoughts from afar. You search out my path and my lying down and are acquainted with all my ways. Even before a word is on my tongue, behold, O LORD, you know it altogether.

You search the heart and test the mind, to give every man according to his ways, according to the fruit of his deeds.

Oh, the depth of the riches and wisdom and knowledge of God! How unsearchable are his judgments and how inscrutable his ways!

Psalm 139:1-4. Jeremiah 17:10. Romans 11:33.

**THUS SAYS THE LORD GOD: . . . I WILL GIVE YOU
A NEW HEART, AND A NEW SPIRIT
I WILL PUT WITHIN YOU.**

I will remove the heart of stone from your flesh and give you a heart of flesh.

Good and upright is the LORD; therefore he instructs sinners in the way. He leads the humble in what is right, and teaches the humble his way. Who is the man who fears the LORD? Him will he instruct in the way that he should choose. His soul shall abide in well-being.

All the paths of the LORD are steadfast love and faithfulness, for those who keep his covenant and his testimonies.

Walk in a manner worthy of the calling to which you have been called, with all humility and gentleness, with patience, bearing with one another in love.

Ezekiel 36:22, 26. Psalm 25:8-9, 12-13. Psalm 25:10. Ephesians 4:1-2.

**DO NOT CONTEND WITH A MAN FOR NO REASON,
WHEN HE HAS DONE YOU NO HARM.**

There are six things that the LORD hates, seven that are an abomination to him: haughty eyes, a lying tongue, and hands that shed innocent blood, a heart that devises wicked plans, feet that make haste to run to evil, a false witness who breathes out lies, and one who sows discord among brothers.

Keep your father's commandment, and forsake not your mother's teaching. Bind them on your heart always; tie them around your neck. When you walk, they will lead you; when you lie down, they will watch over you; and when you awake, they will talk with you.

For the commandment is a lamp and the teaching a light, and the reproofs of discipline are the way of life.

Proverbs 3:30. Proverbs 6:16-23.

BLESSED ARE THE MERCIFUL,
FOR THEY SHALL RECEIVE MERCY.

Bear one another's burdens, and so fulfill the law of Christ.

Whoever pursues righteousness and kindness will find life, righteousness, and honor.

Give to the one who begs from you, and do not refuse the one who would borrow from you.

Rejoice with those who rejoice, weep with those who weep.

Finally, all of you, have unity of mind, sympathy, brotherly love, a tender heart, and a humble mind.

Matthew 5:7. Galatians 6:2. Proverbs 21:21. Matthew 5:42. Romans 12:15.
1 Peter 3:8.

"Bear one another's burdens,
and so fulfill the law of Christ."

BEWARE OF PRACTICING YOUR RIGHTEOUSNESS BEFORE OTHER PEOPLE IN ORDER TO BE SEEN BY THEM, FOR THEN YOU WILL HAVE NO REWARD FROM YOUR FATHER WHO IS IN HEAVEN.

Thus, when you give to the needy, sound no trumpet before you, as the hypocrites do in the synagogues and in the streets, that they may be praised by others. Truly, I say to you, they have received their reward.

But when you give to the needy, do not let your left hand know what your right hand is doing, so that your giving may be in secret. And your Father who sees in secret will reward you.

Matthew 6:1-4.

I WILL GIVE YOU SHEPHERDS AFTER MY OWN HEART, WHO WILL FEED YOU WITH KNOWLEDGE AND UNDERSTANDING.

Respect those who labor among you and are over you in the Lord and admonish you. Esteem them very highly in love because of their work.

Remember your leaders, those who spoke to you the word of God. Consider the outcome of their way of life, and imitate their faith.

Let every person be subject to the governing authorities. For there is no authority except from God, and those that exist have been instituted by God.

Jeremiah 3:15. 1 Thessalonians 5:12-13. Hebrews 13:7. Romans 13:1.

GOD IS YOUR HELPER.

The word of the LORD came to *Jeremiah*, saying, "Before I formed you in the womb I knew you, and before you were born I consecrated you; I appointed you a prophet to the nations."

Then *Jeremiah* said, "Ah, Lord GOD! Behold, I do not know how to speak, for I am only a youth." But the LORD said, "Do not say, 'I am only a youth'; for to all to whom I send you, you shall go, and whatever I command you, you shall speak. Do not be afraid of them, for I am with you to deliver you."

God is able to make all grace abound to you, so that having all sufficiency in all things at all times, you may abound in every good work.

Psalm 54:4. Jeremiah 1:4-8. 2 Corinthians 9:8.

THE LORD IS RIGHTEOUS IN ALL HIS WAYS
AND KIND IN ALL HIS WORKS.

Jabez called upon the God of Israel, saying, "Oh that you would bless me and enlarge my border, and that your hand might be with me, and that you would keep me from harm so that it might not bring me pain!" And God granted what he asked.

God appeared to Solomon, and said to him, "Ask what I shall give you." And Solomon said to God . . . "Give me now wisdom and knowledge . . . for who can govern this people of yours, which is so great?"

Solomon spoke 3,000 proverbs, and his songs were 1,005. He spoke of trees . . . of beasts, and of birds, and of reptiles, and of fish. And people of all nations came to hear the wisdom of Solomon, and from all the kings of the earth, who had heard of his wisdom.

Psalm 145:17. 1 Chronicles 4:10. 2 Chronicles 1:7-8, 10. 1 Kings 4:32-34.

WHERE SHALL WISDOM BE FOUND?
AND WHERE IS THE PLACE OF UNDERSTANDING?

Man does not know its worth, and it is not found in the land of the living.

God understands the way to it, and he knows its place. For he looks to the ends of the earth and sees everything under the heavens.

When he gave to the wind its weight and apportioned the waters by measure, when he made a decree for the rain and a way for the lightning of the thunder, then he saw it and declared it; he established it, and searched it out.

And he said to man, "Behold, the fear of the Lord, that is wisdom, and to turn away from evil is understanding."

Job 28:12-13, 23-28.

PUT NOT YOUR TRUST IN PRINCES, IN A SON OF MAN,
IN WHOM THERE IS NO SALVATION.

When his breath departs, he returns to the earth; on that very day his plans perish. Blessed is he whose help is the God of Jacob, whose hope is in the LORD his God, who made heaven and earth, the sea, and all that is in them, who keeps faith forever; who executes justice for the oppressed, who gives food to the hungry.

Fear not, for I am with you; be not dismayed, for I am your God; I will strengthen you, I will help you, I will uphold you with my righteous right hand.

For I, the LORD your God, hold your right hand; it is I who say to you, "Fear not, I am the one who helps you."

Psalm 146:3. Psalm 146:4-7. Isaiah 41:10, 13.

DO NOT LOSE SIGHT OF THESE—KEEP SOUND WISDOM AND DISCRETION.

I have taught you the way of wisdom; I have led you in the paths of uprightness. When you walk, your step will not be hampered, and if you run, you will not stumble. Keep hold of instruction; do not let go; guard her, for she is your life. Do not enter the path of the wicked, and do not walk in the way of the evil. Avoid it; do not go on it; turn away from it and pass on.

But the path of the righteous is like the light of dawn, which shines brighter and brighter until full day.

Let your eyes look directly forward, and your gaze be straight before you. Ponder the path of your feet; then all your ways will be sure.

Proverbs 3:21. Proverbs 4:11-15, 18, 25-26.

GOD IS WITH US.

If God is for us, who can be against us?

The LORD is on my side; I will not fear. What can man do to me?

The LORD is my light and my salvation; whom shall I fear? The LORD is the stronghold of my life; of whom shall I be afraid?

Though an army encamp against me, my heart shall not fear; though war arise against me, yet I will be confident.

The LORD of hosts is with us; the God of Jacob is our fortress.

Isaiah 8:10. Romans 8:31. Psalm 118:6. Psalm 27:1, 3. Psalm 46:7.

WHEN YOU LIE DOWN,
YOUR SLEEP WILL BE SWEET.

One day *Jesus* got into a boat with his disciples, and he said to them, "Let us go across to the other side of the lake." So they set out, and as they sailed he fell asleep. A windstorm came down on the lake, and they were filling with water and were in danger. *The disciples* went and woke him, saying, "Master, Master, we are perishing!" He awoke and rebuked the wind and the raging waves, and they ceased, and there was a calm.

Jesus said to them, "Where is your faith?" They were afraid, and they marveled, saying to one another, "Who then is this, that he commands even winds and water, and they obey him?"

In peace I will both lie down and sleep; for you alone, O LORD, make me dwell in safety.

Proverbs 3:24. Luke 8:22-25. Psalm 4:8.

"The Lord will instruct you and teach you in the way you should go; he will counsel you with his eye upon you."

YOUR WORD IS A LAMP TO MY FEET
AND A LIGHT TO MY PATH.

The L*ORD* will instruct you and teach you in the way you should go; *he* will counsel you with *his* eye upon you. Be not like a horse or a mule, without understanding, which must be curbed with bit and bridle, or it will not stay near you.

All the paths of the L*ORD* are steadfast love and faithfulness, for those who keep his covenant and his testimonies.

Make me to know your ways, O L*ORD*; teach me your paths.

Psalm 119:105. Psalm 32:8-9. Psalm 25:10. Psalm 25:4.

IN YOUR HEARTS HONOR CHRIST THE LORD AS HOLY,
ALWAYS BEING PREPARED TO MAKE A DEFENSE
TO ANYONE WHO ASKS YOU FOR A REASON
FOR THE HOPE THAT IS IN YOU.

If anyone suffers as a Christian, let him not be ashamed, but let him glorify God in that name.

For this is a gracious thing, when, mindful of God, one endures sorrows while suffering unjustly. For what credit is it if, when you sin and are beaten for it, you endure? But if when you do good and suffer for it you endure, this is a gracious thing in the sight of God.

Whatever good anyone does, this he will receive back from the Lord.

1 Peter 3:15. 1 Peter 4:16. 1 Peter 2:19-20. Ephesians 6:8.

EXECUTE JUSTICE AND RIGHTEOUSNESS.

Daniel became distinguished above all the other presidents and satraps, because an excellent spirit was in him. And the king planned to set him over the whole kingdom. Then the presidents and the satraps sought to find a ground for complaint against Daniel with regard to the kingdom, but they could find no ground for complaint or any fault, because he was faithful, and no error or fault was found in him.

So this Daniel prospered during the reign of Darius and the reign of Cyrus the Persian.

Hear what the LORD says: . . . "He has told you, O man, what is good; and what does the LORD require of you but to do justice, and to love kindness, and to walk humbly with your God?"

Ezekiel 45:9. Daniel 6:3-4, 28. Micah 6:1, 8.

EVEN A CHILD MAKES HIMSELF KNOWN
BY HIS ACTS, BY WHETHER HIS CONDUCT IS PURE
AND UPRIGHT.

Remember also your Creator in the days of your youth.

Honor your father and your mother, that your days may be long in the land that the LORD your God is giving you.

Be imitators of God, as beloved children. And walk in love, as Christ loved us and gave himself up for us, a fragrant offering and sacrifice to God.

But you, beloved, building yourselves up in your most holy faith and praying in the Holy Spirit, keep yourselves in the love of God, waiting for the mercy of our Lord Jesus Christ that leads to eternal life.

Proverbs 20:11. Ecclesiastes 12:1. Exodus 20:12. Ephesians 5:1-2. Jude 20-21.

I URGE THAT SUPPLICATIONS, PRAYERS, INTERCESSIONS, AND THANKSGIVINGS BE MADE FOR ALL PEOPLE—

—for kings and all who are in high positions, that we may lead a peaceful and quiet life, godly and dignified in every way.

This is good, and it is pleasing in the sight of God our Savior, who desires all people to be saved and to come to the knowledge of the truth.

For there is one God, and there is one mediator between God and men, the man Christ Jesus, who gave himself as a ransom for all.

1 Timothy 2:1-6.

THE LORD PRESERVES THE FAITHFUL.

Preserve me, O God, for in you I take refuge. I say to the LORD, "You are my Lord; I have no good apart from you."

I bless the LORD who gives me counsel; in the night also my heart instructs me. I have set the LORD always before me; because he is at my right hand, I shall not be shaken.

You make known to me the path of life; in your presence there is fullness of joy; at your right hand are pleasures forevermore.

Psalm 31:23. Psalm 16:1-2, 7-8, 11.

THE LORD IS ON YOUR SIDE AS YOUR HELPER.

No temptation has overtaken you that is not common to man. God is faithful, and he will not let you be tempted beyond your ability, but with the temptation he will also provide the way of escape, that you may be able to endure it.

Count it all joy when you meet trials of various kinds, for you know that the testing of your faith produces steadfastness. And let steadfastness have its full effect, that you may be perfect and complete, lacking in nothing.

Blessed is the man who remains steadfast under trial, for when he has stood the test he will receive the crown of life, which God has promised to those who love him.

Be sober-minded; be watchful. Your adversary the devil prowls around like a roaring lion, seeking someone to devour. Resist him.

Psalm 118:7. 1 Corinthians 10:13. James 1:2-4, 12. 1 Peter 5:8-9.

MY HELP COMES FROM THE LORD, WHO MADE
HEAVEN AND EARTH.

As the mountains surround Jerusalem, so the LORD surrounds his people, from this time forth and forevermore.

The LORD will guide you continually and satisfy your desire in scorched places and make your bones strong; and you shall be like a watered garden, like a spring of water, whose waters do not fail.

To you I lift up my eyes, O you who are enthroned in the heavens! Behold, as the eyes of servants look to the hand of their master, as the eyes of a maidservant to the hand of her mistress, so *my* eyes look to the LORD *my* God.

My eyes are ever toward the LORD, for he will pluck my feet out of the net.

My help is in the name of the LORD, who made heaven and earth.

Psalm 121:2. Psalm 125:2. Isaiah 58:11. Psalm 123:1-2. Psalm 25:15. Psalm 124:8.

O LORD, YOU ARE OUR FATHER; WE ARE THE CLAY, AND YOU ARE OUR POTTER; WE ARE ALL THE WORK OF YOUR HAND.

Oh that you would rend the heavens and come down, that the mountains might quake at your presence—as when fire kindles brushwood and the fire causes water to boil—to make your name known to your adversaries, and that the nations might tremble at your presence!

When you did awesome things that we did not look for, you came down, the mountains quaked at your presence. From of old no one has heard or perceived by the ear, no eye has seen a God besides you, who acts for those who wait for him.

You meet him who joyfully works righteousness, those who remember you in your ways.

Isaiah 64:8. Isaiah 64:1-5.

IS ANYTHING TOO HARD FOR THE LORD?

Nebuchadnezzar in furious rage commanded that Shadrach, Meshach, and Abednego be brought . . . and said to them, "Is it true, O Shadrach, Meshach, and Abednego, that you do not serve my gods or worship the golden image that I have set up? Now . . . if you do not worship, you shall immediately be cast into a burning fiery furnace. And who is the god who will deliver you out of my hands?"

Shadrach, Meshach, and Abednego answered and said to the king, "O Nebuchadnezzar, we have no need to answer you in this matter. If this be so, our God whom we serve is able to deliver us from the burning fiery furnace, and he will deliver us out of your hand, O king."

Shadrach, Meshach, and Abednego came out from the fire. . . . The hair of their heads was not singed, their cloaks were not harmed, and no smell of fire had come upon them.

Genesis 18:14. Daniel 3:13-17, 26-27.

BY FAITH THE PEOPLE OF OLD
RECEIVED THEIR COMMENDATION.

By faith Noah, being warned by God concerning events as yet unseen, in reverent fear constructed an ark for the saving of his household. By this he condemned the world and became an heir of the righteousness that comes by faith.

By faith Abraham obeyed when he was called to go out to a place that he was to receive as an inheritance. And he went out, not knowing where he was going. By faith Moses, when he was born, was hidden for three months by his parents, because they saw that the child was beautiful, and they were not afraid of the king's edict. By faith the walls of Jericho fell down after they had been encircled for seven days.

Let us run with endurance the race that is set before us.

Hebrews 11:2, 7-8, 23, 29-30. Hebrews 12:1.

FAITH IS THE ASSURANCE OF THINGS HOPED FOR,
THE CONVICTION OF THINGS NOT SEEN.

By faith Moses, when he was grown up, refused to be called the son of Pharaoh's daughter, choosing rather to be mistreated with the people of God than to enjoy the fleeting pleasures of sin. He considered the reproach of Christ greater wealth than the treasures of Egypt, for he was looking to the reward.

Time would fail me to tell of Gideon, Barak, Samson, Jephthah, of David and Samuel and the prophets—who through faith conquered kingdoms, enforced justice, obtained promises, stopped the mouths of lions, quenched the power of fire, escaped the edge of the sword, were made strong out of weakness, became mighty in war, put foreign armies to flight. Without faith it is impossible to please him, for whoever would draw near to God must believe that he exists and that he rewards those who seek him.

Hebrews 11:1, 24-26, 32-34. Hebrews 11:6.

WHAT CAUSES QUARRELS AND
WHAT CAUSES FIGHTS AMONG YOU?

God opposes the proud, but gives grace to the humble. Submit yourselves therefore to God. Resist the devil, and he will flee from you.

Draw near to God, and he will draw near to you. Cleanse your hands, you sinners, and purify your hearts, you double-minded. Do not speak evil against one another.

Repent . . . and turn again, that your sins may be blotted out, that times of refreshing may come from the presence of the Lord,

Humble yourselves before the Lord, and he will exalt you.

James 4:1, 6, 7, 8, 11. Acts 3:19, 20. James 4:10.

"Draw near to God,
and he will draw near to you."

SURELY THERE IS NOT A RIGHTEOUS MAN ON EARTH WHO DOES GOOD AND NEVER SINS.

None is righteous, no, not one; no one understands; no one seeks for God.

All have turned aside; together they have become worthless; no one does good, not even one.

Christ himself bore our sins in his body on the tree, that we might die to sin and live to righteousness. By his wounds *we* have been healed.

For by works of the law no human being will be justified in *God's* sight, since through the law comes knowledge of sin. All . . . are justified by his grace as a gift, through the redemption that is in Christ Jesus.

Ecclesiastes 7:20. Romans 3:10-12. 1 Peter 2:24. Romans 3:20, 23-24.

BLESSED IS THE MAN AGAINST WHOM THE LORD COUNTS NO INIQUITY, AND IN WHOSE SPIRIT THERE IS NO DECEIT.

Since we have been justified by faith, we have peace with God through our Lord Jesus Christ. Through him we have also obtained access by faith into this grace in which we stand, and we rejoice in hope of the glory of God.

From him and through him and to him are all things. To him be glory forever. Amen.

Psalm 32:2. Romans 5:1-2. Romans 11:36.

EVERYONE WHO BELIEVES THAT JESUS IS THE CHRIST HAS BEEN BORN OF GOD, AND EVERYONE WHO LOVES THE FATHER LOVES WHOEVER HAS BEEN BORN OF HIM.

By this we know that we love the children of God, when we love God and obey his commandments. For this is the love of God, that we keep his commandments. And his commandments are not burdensome.

For everyone who has been born of God overcomes the world. And this is the victory that has overcome the world—our faith. Who is it that overcomes the world except the one who believes that Jesus is the Son of God?

1 John 5:1-5.

SINCE THEN WE HAVE A GREAT HIGH PRIEST WHO HAS PASSED THROUGH THE HEAVENS, JESUS, THE SON OF GOD, LET US HOLD FAST OUR CONFESSION.

For we do not have a high priest who is unable to sympathize with our weaknesses, but one who in every respect has been tempted as we are, yet without sin. Let us then with confidence draw near to the throne of grace, that we may receive mercy and find grace to help in time of need.

For the LORD is good; his steadfast love endures forever, and his faithfulness to all generations.

Hebrews 4:14-16. Psalm 100:5.

KNOW THE LOVE OF CHRIST THAT
SURPASSES KNOWLEDGE.

Be strengthened with power through his Spirit in your inner being, so that Christ may dwell in your hearts through faith—that you, being rooted and grounded in love, may have strength to comprehend . . . the love of Christ that surpasses knowledge.

For you know the grace of our Lord Jesus Christ, that though he was rich, yet for your sake he became poor, so that you by his poverty might become rich.

Beloved, if God so loved *you, you* also ought to love one another.

Be kind to one another, tenderhearted, forgiving one another, as God in Christ forgave you.

Ephesians 3:19. Ephesians 3:16-19. 2 Corinthians 8:9. 1 John 4:11. Ephesians 4:32.

BLESS THOSE WHO PERSECUTE YOU;
BLESS AND DO NOT CURSE THEM.

Do all things without grumbling or questioning, that you may be blameless and innocent, children of God without blemish in the midst of a crooked and twisted generation, among whom you shine as lights in the world.

Do it with gentleness and respect, having a good conscience, so that, when you are slandered, those who revile your good behavior in Christ may be put to shame.

Romans 12:14. Philippians 2:14-15. 1 Peter 3:15-16.

LOVE YOUR ENEMIES AND PRAY FOR THOSE WHO PERSECUTE YOU.

[The Jewish leaders] . . . were enraged, and they ground their teeth at Stephen. But he, full of the Holy Spirit, gazed into heaven and saw the glory of God, and Jesus standing at the right hand of God.

They cried out with a loud voice and stopped their ears and rushed together at him.

Then they cast him out of the city and stoned him. . . . As they were stoning Stephen, he called out, "Lord Jesus, receive my spirit." And falling to his knees he cried out with a loud voice, "Lord, do not hold this sin against them."

Matthew 5:44. Acts 7:54-55, 57-60.

THE FRUIT OF THE SPIRIT IS LOVE, JOY, PEACE, PATIENCE, KINDNESS, GOODNESS, FAITHFULNESS, GENTLENESS, SELF-CONTROL.

Do not lie to one another, seeing that you have put off the old self with its practices and have put on the new self, which is being renewed in knowledge after the image of its creator.

Lying lips are an abomination to the LORD, but those who act faithfully are his delight.

Do not grow weary of doing good, for in due season *you* will reap, if *you* do not give up.

Be patient. Establish your hearts, for the coming of the Lord is at hand.

Galatians 5:22-23. Colossians 3:9-10. Proverbs 12:22. Galatians 6:9. James 5:8.

IF POSSIBLE, SO FAR AS IT DEPENDS ON YOU, LIVE PEACEABLY WITH ALL.

Isaac dug again the wells of water that had been dug in the days of Abraham his father. . . . But when Isaac's servants dug in the valley and found there a well of spring water, the herdsmen of Gerar quarreled with Isaac's herdsmen, saying, "The water is ours.". . .

Then they dug another well, and they quarreled over that also. . . . He moved from there and dug another well, and they did not quarrel over it. So he . . . [said], "Now the LORD has made room for us, and we shall be fruitful in the land."

Repay no one evil for evil, but give thought to do what is honorable in the sight of all.

Romans 12:18. Genesis 26:18-22. Romans 12:17.

ENCOURAGE ONE ANOTHER.

Be on guard, keep awake.

Seek the things that are above, where Christ is, seated at the right hand of God. When Christ who is your life appears, then you also will appear with him in glory.

The one who conquers will be clothed thus in white garments.

For the trumpet will sound, and the dead will be raised imperishable, and we shall be changed.

But concerning that day or that hour, no one knows, not even the angels in heaven, nor the Son, but only the Father.

1 Thessalonians 4:18. Mark 13:33. Colossians 3:1, 4. Revelation 3:5.
1 Corinthians 15:52. Mark 13:32.

THE NEW WAY OF THE SPIRIT.

Do not be conformed to this world, but be transformed by the renewal of your mind, that by testing you may discern what is the will of God, what is good and acceptable and perfect.

Put on the new self, created after the likeness of God in true righteousness and holiness.

Admonish the idle, encourage the fainthearted, help the weak, be patient with them all. . . . Always seek to do good to one another and to everyone. Rejoice always, pray without ceasing, give thanks in all circumstances; for this is the will of God in Christ Jesus for you.

Romans 7:6. Romans 12:2. Ephesians 4:24. 1 Thessalonians 5:14-18.

HALLELUJAH! FOR THE LORD OUR GOD
THE ALMIGHTY REIGNS.

What is impossible with men is possible with God.

All the inhabitants of the earth are accounted as nothing, and *God* does according to his will among the host of heaven and among the inhabitants of the earth; and none can stay his hand or say to him, "What have you done?"

There is none who can deliver from *his* hand; *he works*, and who can turn it back?

I will hope continually and will praise you yet more and more. My mouth will tell of your righteous acts, of your deeds of salvation all the day, for their number is past my knowledge.

I know that *God* can do all things, and that no purpose of *his* can be thwarted.

Revelation 19:6. Luke 18:27. Daniel 4:35. Isaiah 43:13. Psalm 71:14-15. Job 42:2.

YOUR STEADFAST LOVE, O LORD, EXTENDS TO THE HEAVENS, YOUR FAITHFULNESS TO THE CLOUDS.

The LORD is merciful and gracious, slow to anger and abounding in steadfast love. He will not always chide, nor will he keep his anger forever. He does not deal with us according to our sins, nor repay us according to our iniquities.

For as high as the heavens are above the earth, so great is his steadfast love toward those who fear him; as far as the east is from the west, so far does he remove our transgressions from us.

As a father shows compassion to his children, so the LORD shows compassion to those who fear him.

Psalm 36:5. Psalm 103:8-13.

"As a father shows compassion to his children, so the LORD shows compassion to those who fear him."

WHO IS THE LORD?

Thus says the LORD, he who created you, O Jacob, he who formed you, O Israel: "Fear not, for I have redeemed you; I have called you by name, you are mine. . . . I, I am the LORD, and besides me there is no savior."

Thus says the LORD, the Holy One of Israel . . . "I made the earth and created man on it; it was my hands that stretched out the heavens, and I commanded all their host."

"Turn to me and be saved, all the ends of the earth! For I am God, and there is no other. By myself I have sworn; from my mouth has gone out in righteousness a word that shall not return: To me every knee shall bow, every tongue shall swear allegiance."

Exodus 5:2. Isaiah 43:1, 11. Isaiah 45:11-12, 22-23.

THE LORD WENT BEFORE THEM BY DAY IN A PILLAR OF CLOUD TO LEAD THEM ALONG THE WAY, AND BY NIGHT IN A PILLAR OF FIRE TO GIVE THEM LIGHT, THAT THEY MIGHT TRAVEL BY DAY AND BY NIGHT.

When Pharaoh let the people [of Israel] go, God did not lead them by way of the land of the Philistines, although that was near. . . . But God led the people around by the way of the wilderness toward the Red Sea.

My thoughts are not your thoughts, neither are your ways my ways, declares the LORD. For as the heavens are higher than the earth, so are my ways higher than your ways and my thoughts than your thoughts.

He will guide us forever.

Exodus 13:21. Exodus 13:17-18. Isaiah 55:8-9. Psalm 48:14.

THE LORD SITS ENTHRONED OVER THE FLOOD; THE LORD SITS ENTHRONED AS KING FOREVER.

The earth was corrupt in God's sight, and the earth was filled with violence. And God saw the earth, and behold, it was corrupt, for all flesh had corrupted their way on the earth.

And God said to Noah . . . , "Make yourself an ark of gopher wood. . . . I will bring a flood of waters upon the earth to destroy all flesh in which is the breath of life under heaven. Everything that is on the earth shall die. But I will establish my covenant with you, and you shall come into the ark, you, your sons, your wife, and your sons' wives with you."

The LORD's curse is on the house of the wicked, but he blesses the dwelling of the righteous.

Psalm 29:10. Genesis 6:11-14, 17-18. Proverbs 3:33.

GOD'S EYES ARE ON THE WAYS OF A MAN, AND HE SEES ALL HIS STEPS.

Ah, you who hide deep from the LORD your counsel, whose deeds are in the dark, and who say, "Who sees us? Who knows us?"

You turn things upside down! Shall the potter be regarded as the clay, that the thing made should say of its maker, "He did not make me"; or the thing formed say of him who formed it, "He has no understanding"?

Job 34:21. Isaiah 29:15-16.

A DREAM COMES WITH MUCH BUSINESS, AND A FOOL'S VOICE WITH MANY WORDS.

When you vow a vow to God, do not delay paying it, for he has no pleasure in fools. Pay what you vow. It is better that you should not vow than that you should vow and not pay. For when dreams increase and words grow many, there is vanity; but God is the one you must fear.

Whoever keeps his mouth and his tongue keeps himself out of trouble.

Whoever guards his mouth preserves his life; he who opens wide his lips comes to ruin.

Whoever desires to love life and see good days, let him keep his tongue from evil and his lips from speaking deceit.

Ecclesiastes 5:3-5, 7. Proverbs 21:23. Proverbs 13:3. 1 Peter 3:10.

GUARD YOUR STEPS WHEN YOU GO TO THE HOUSE OF GOD.

Be not rash with your mouth, nor let your heart be hasty to utter a word before God, for God is in heaven and you are on earth. Therefore let your words be few.

Let every person be quick to hear, slow to speak, slow to anger.

Not everyone who says to me, "Lord, Lord," will enter the kingdom of heaven, but the one who does the will of my Father who is in heaven.

Everyone then who hears these words of mine and does them will be like a wise man who built his house on the rock.

Ecclesiastes 5:1-2. James 1:19. Matthew 7:21, 24.

I CLING TO YOUR TESTIMONIES, O LORD;
LET ME NOT BE PUT TO SHAME!

Create in me a clean heart, O God, and renew a right spirit within me. Restore to me the joy of your salvation, and uphold me with a willing spirit.

Who can discern his errors? Declare me innocent from hidden faults. Keep back your servant also from presumptuous sins; let them not have dominion over me! Then I shall be blameless, and innocent of great transgression. Let the words of my mouth and the meditation of my heart be acceptable in your sight, O LORD, my rock and my redeemer.

Psalm 119:31. Psalm 51:10, 12. Psalm 19:12-14.

INCLINE MY HEART TO YOUR TESTIMONIES,
AND NOT TO SELFISH GAIN!

Blessed are you, O LORD; teach me your statutes!

With my lips I declare all the rules of your mouth. In the way of your testimonies I delight as much as in all riches. I will meditate on your precepts and fix my eyes on your ways. I will delight in your statutes; I will not forget your word.

Deal bountifully with your servant, that I may live and keep your word. Open my eyes, that I may behold wondrous things out of your law. I am a sojourner on the earth; hide not your commandments from me!

Psalm 119:36. Psalm 119:12-19.

I CONSIDER ALL YOUR PRECEPTS TO BE RIGHT; I HATE EVERY FALSE WAY.

The law of the LORD is perfect, reviving the soul; the testimony of the LORD is sure, making wise the simple; the precepts of the LORD are right, rejoicing the heart; the commandment of the LORD is pure, enlightening the eyes; the fear of the LORD is clean, enduring forever; the rules of the LORD are true, and righteous altogether. More to be desired are they than gold, even much fine gold; sweeter also than honey and drippings of the honeycomb.

Finally . . . whatever is true, whatever is honorable, whatever is just, whatever is pure, whatever is lovely, whatever is commendable, if there is any excellence, if there is anything worthy of praise, think about these things.

This God—his way is perfect; the word of the LORD proves true.

Psalm 119:128. Psalm 19:7-10. Philippians 4:8. Psalm 18:30.

THE WORD OF GOD IS LIVING AND ACTIVE.

Oh how I love your law! It is my meditation all the day. Your commandment makes me wiser than my enemies, for it is ever with me.

I hold back my feet from every evil way, in order to keep your word. I do not turn aside from your rules, for you have taught me.

How sweet are your words to my taste, sweeter than honey to my mouth! Through your precepts I get understanding; therefore I hate every false way.

Your testimonies are my heritage forever, for they are the joy of my heart.

Hebrews 4:12. Psalm 119:97-98, 101-104, 111.

THROUGH LOVE SERVE ONE ANOTHER.

The whole law is fulfilled in one [command]: "You shall love your neighbor as yourself." But if you bite and devour one another, watch out that you are not consumed by one another.

The beginning of strife is like letting out water, so quit before the quarrel breaks out.

I say, walk by the Spirit, and you will not gratify the desires of the flesh. For the desires of the flesh are against the Spirit, and the desires of the Spirit are against the flesh, for these are opposed to each other, to keep you from doing the things you want to do.

Galatians 5:13-15. Proverbs 17:14. Galatians 5:16-17.

TAKE NO PART IN THE UNFRUITFUL WORKS
OF DARKNESS, BUT INSTEAD EXPOSE THEM.

Now the works of the flesh are evident: . . .
strife
jealousy
fits of anger
rivalries . . .
divisions
envy
drunkenness . . . and things like these. . . .
Those who do such things will not inherit the kingdom of God. For it is shameful even to speak of the things that they do in secret.

Ephesians 5:11. Galatians 5:19-21. Ephesians 5:12.

TEACH US TO NUMBER OUR DAYS THAT WE MAY GET A HEART OF WISDOM.

Look carefully then how you walk, not as unwise but as wise, making the best use of the time.

Only be very careful to observe the commandment and the law that Moses the servant of the LORD commanded you, to love the LORD your God, and to walk in all his ways and to keep his commandments and to cling to him and to serve him with all your heart and with all your soul.

Be all the more diligent to make your calling and election sure, for if you practice these qualities you will never fall. For in this way there will be richly provided for you an entrance into the eternal kingdom of our Lord and Savior Jesus Christ.

Psalm 90:12. Ephesians 5:15-16. Joshua 22:5. 2 Peter 1:10-11.

IN MY FATHER'S HOUSE ARE MANY ROOMS. IF IT WERE NOT SO, WOULD I HAVE TOLD YOU THAT I GO TO PREPARE A PLACE FOR YOU?

And if I go and prepare a place for you, I will come again and will take you to myself, that where I am you may be also.

The city has no need of sun or moon to shine on it, for the glory of God gives it light, and its lamp is the Lamb. By its light will the nations walk, and the kings of the earth will bring their glory into it, and its gates will never be shut by day—and there will be no night there.

Nothing unclean will ever enter it, nor anyone who does what is detestable or false, but only those who are written in the Lamb's book of life.

John 14:2-3. Revelation 21:23-25, 27.

RECEIVE WITH MEEKNESS THE IMPLANTED WORD, WHICH IS ABLE TO SAVE YOUR SOULS.

Be doers of the word, and not hearers only, deceiving yourselves.

For if anyone is a hearer of the word and not a doer, he is like a man who looks intently at his natural face in a mirror. For he looks at himself and goes away and at once forgets what he was like.

But the one who . . . perseveres, being no hearer who forgets but a doer who acts, he will be blessed in his doing.

James 1:21-25.

HONOR YOUR FATHER AND YOUR MOTHER, THAT YOUR DAYS MAY BE LONG IN THE LAND THAT THE LORD YOUR GOD IS GIVING YOU.

Children, obey your parents in the Lord, for this is right.

Whoever ignores instruction despises himself, but he who listens to reproof gains intelligence.

Good sense is a fountain of life to him who has it.

Hear . . . your father's instruction, and forsake not your mother's teaching, for they are a graceful garland for your head and pendants for your neck.

Exodus 20:12. Ephesians 6:1. Proverbs 15:32. Proverbs 16:22. Proverbs 1:8-9.

DO NOTHING FROM RIVALRY OR CONCEIT, BUT IN HUMILITY COUNT OTHERS MORE SIGNIFICANT THAN YOURSELVES.

Thus says the One who is high and lifted up, who inhabits eternity, whose name is Holy: "I dwell in the high and holy place, and also with him who is of a contrite and lowly spirit."

Let no one deceive himself. If anyone among you thinks that he is wise in this age, let him become a fool that he may become wise.

Let another praise you, and not your own mouth.

The reward for humility and fear of the LORD is riches and honor and life.

So do not become proud.

Whoever exalts himself will be humbled, and whoever humbles himself will be exalted.

Philippians 2:3. Isaiah 57:15. 1 Corinthians 3:18. Proverbs 27:2. Proverbs 22:4.
Romans 11:20. Matthew 23:12.

KEEP YOURSELVES FROM IDOLS.

For the grace of God has appeared, bringing salvation for all people, training us to renounce ungodliness and worldly passions, and to live self-controlled, upright, and godly lives in the present age.

You are the light of the world. A city set on a hill cannot be hidden. Nor do people light a lamp and put it under a basket, but on a stand, and it gives light to all in the house.

In the same way, let your light shine before others, so that they may see your good works and give glory to your Father who is in heaven.

1 John 5:21. Titus 2:11-12. Matthew 5:14-16.

IF ANY OF YOU LACKS WISDOM, LET HIM ASK GOD, WHO GIVES GENEROUSLY TO ALL WITHOUT REPROACH, AND IT WILL BE GIVEN HIM.

But let him ask in faith, with no doubting, for the one who doubts is like a wave of the sea that is driven and tossed by the wind.

Have you not known? Have you not heard? The LORD is the everlasting God, the Creator of the ends of the earth. He does not faint or grow weary; his understanding is unsearchable.

Let us draw near with a true heart in full assurance of faith.

James 1:5-6. Isaiah 40:28. Hebrews 10:22.

THE LORD SURROUNDS HIS PEOPLE.

Asa went out to meet [Zerah the Ethiopian], and they drew up their lines of battle in the Valley of Zephathah at Mareshah. And Asa cried to the LORD his God, "O LORD, there is none like you to help, between the mighty and the weak. Help us, O LORD our God, for we rely on you, and in your name we have come against this multitude. O LORD, you are our God; let not man prevail against you." So the LORD defeated the Ethiopians before Asa and before Judah, and the Ethiopians fled.

Who is this King of glory? The LORD, strong and mighty, the LORD, mighty in battle!

The LORD is the strength of his people.

Psalm 125:2. 2 Chronicles 14:10-12. Psalm 24:8. Psalm 28:8.

OH, THE DEPTH OF THE RICHES AND WISDOM AND KNOWLEDGE OF GOD!

How unsearchable are his judgments and how inscrutable his ways! For who has known the mind of the Lord, or who has been his counselor? Or who has given a gift to him that he might be repaid?

The LORD by wisdom founded the earth; by understanding he established the heavens; by his knowledge the deeps broke open, and the clouds drop down the dew.

O King of the nations . . . among all the wise ones of the nations and in all their kingdoms there is none like you.

The LORD searches all hearts and understands every plan and thought.

Your Father knows what you need before you ask him.

He knows everything.

Blessed be the name of God forever and ever, to whom belong wisdom and might.

Romans 11:33-35. Proverbs 3:19-20. Jeremiah 10:7. 1 Chronicles 28:9. Matthew 6:8. 1 John 3:20. Daniel 2:20.

THE BATTLE IS THE LORD'S.

David said to Saul, "Let no man's heart fail because of [Goliath]. Your servant will go and fight with this Philistine." Then he took his staff in his hand and chose five smooth stones from the brook and put them in his shepherd's pouch. His sling was in his hand, and he approached the Philistine. And the Philistine moved forward and came near to David, with his shield-bearer in front of him.

Then David said to the Philistine, "You come to me with a sword and with a spear and with a javelin, but I come to you in the name of the LORD of hosts, the God of the armies of Israel, whom you have defied. The LORD saves not with sword and spear. The battle is the LORD's, and he will give you into our hand." So David prevailed over the Philistine with a sling and with a stone. Our sufficiency is from God.

1 Samuel 17:47. 1 Samuel 17:32, 40-41, 45, 47, 50. 2 Corinthians 3:5.

SUFFERING PRODUCES ENDURANCE, AND ENDURANCE PRODUCES CHARACTER, AND CHARACTER PRODUCES HOPE.

God is treating *us* as sons. For what son is there whom his father does not discipline? If *we* are left without discipline, in which all have participated, then *we* are illegitimate children and not sons.

We have had earthly fathers who disciplined us and we respected them. Shall we not much more be subject to the Father of spirits and live? For they disciplined us for a short time as it seemed best to them, but [God] disciplines us for our good, that we may share his holiness.

For the moment all discipline seems painful rather than pleasant, but later it yields the peaceful fruit of righteousness to those who have been trained by it.

Romans 5:3-4. Hebrews 12:7-11.

GREAT IS THE LORD!

Blessed is he whose help is the God of Jacob, whose hope is in the LORD his God, who made heaven and earth, the sea, and all that is in them, who keeps faith forever; who executes justice for the oppressed, who gives food to the hungry.

The LORD sets the prisoners free; the LORD opens the eyes of the blind. The LORD lifts up those who are bowed down; the LORD loves the righteous.

The LORD watches over the sojourners; he upholds the widow and the fatherless, but the way of the wicked he brings to ruin.

The LORD will reign forever, your God, O Zion, to all generations. Praise the LORD!

Malachi 1:5. Psalm 146:5-10.

IN THE LAST DAYS THERE WILL COME TIMES OF DIFFICULTY.

For people will be lovers of self, lovers of money, proud, arrogant, abusive, disobedient to their parents, ungrateful, unholy, heartless, unappeasable, slanderous, without self-control, brutal, not loving good, treacherous, reckless, swollen with conceit, lovers of pleasure rather than lovers of God, having the appearance of godliness, but denying its power. Avoid such people.

Continue in what you have learned and have firmly believed, knowing from whom you learned it and how from childhood you have been acquainted with the sacred writings, which are able to make you wise for salvation through faith in Christ Jesus.

All Scripture is breathed out by God and profitable for teaching, for reproof, for correction, and for training in righteousness, that the man of God may be competent, equipped for every good work.

2 Timothy 3:1-5, 14-17.

TEACHER, WHICH IS THE GREAT COMMANDMENT IN THE LAW?

[Jesus] said to him, "You shall love the Lord your God with all your heart and with all your soul and with all your mind. This is the great and first commandment. And a second is like it: You shall love your neighbor as yourself."

Owe no one anything, except to love each other, for the one who loves another has fulfilled the law. For the commandments, "You shall not commit adultery, You shall not murder, You shall not steal, You shall not covet," and any other commandment, are summed up in this word: "You shall love your neighbor as yourself."

Love does no wrong to a neighbor; therefore love is the fulfilling of the law.

Matthew 22:36-39. Romans 13:8-10.

AS CHARCOAL TO HOT EMBERS AND WOOD TO FIRE, SO IS A QUARRELSOME MAN FOR KINDLING STRIFE.

Whoever belittles his neighbor lacks sense, but a man of understanding remains silent.

The tongue is a small member, yet it boasts of great things. How great a forest is set ablaze by such a small fire! And the tongue is a fire, a world of unrighteousness. The tongue is set among our members, staining the whole body, setting on fire the entire course of life. . . . Every kind of beast and bird, of reptile and sea creature, can be tamed and has been tamed by mankind, but no human being can tame the tongue. It is a restless evil, full of deadly poison.

Submit yourselves therefore to God. Resist the devil, and he will flee from you. Draw near to God, and he will draw near to you.

Proverbs 26:21. Proverbs 11:12. James 3:5-8. James 4:7-8.

DO NOT GO ON SINNING.

Turn from all your transgressions, lest iniquity be your ruin. Cast away from you all the transgressions that you have committed, and make yourselves a new heart and a new spirit!

So put away all malice and all deceit and hypocrisy and envy and all slander.

Put on the whole armor of God . . . the belt of truth . . . the breastplate of righteousness . . . the gospel of peace . . . the shield of faith . . . the helmet of salvation . . . the sword of the Spirit, which is the word of God, praying at all times in the Spirit. . . . Keep alert with all perseverance.

1 Corinthians 15:34. Ezekiel 18:30-31. 1 Peter 2:1. Ephesians 6:11, 14-18.

BY THIS WE KNOW LOVE, THAT [CHRIST] LAID DOWN HIS LIFE FOR US.

God shows his love for us in that while we were still sinners, Christ died for us.

He himself bore our sins in his body on the tree, that we might die to sin and live to righteousness. By his wounds you have been healed.

He was oppressed, and he was afflicted, yet he opened not his mouth; like a lamb that is led to the slaughter, and like a sheep that before its shearers is silent, so he opened not his mouth.

He humbled himself by becoming obedient to the point of death, even death on a cross.

Consider him who endured from sinners such hostility against himself, so that you may not grow weary or fainthearted.

1 John 3:16. Romans 5:8. 1 Peter 2:24. Isaiah 53:7. Philippians 2:8. Hebrews 12:3.

PILATE TOOK JESUS AND FLOGGED HIM.

And the soldiers twisted together a crown of thorns and put it on his head and arrayed him in a purple robe. They came up to him, saying, "Hail, King of the Jews!" and struck him with their hands.

When the chief priests and the officers saw him, they cried out, "Crucify him, crucify him!"

He was wounded for our transgressions; he was crushed for our iniquities; upon him was the chastisement that brought us peace, and with his stripes we are healed.

All we like sheep have gone astray; we have turned—every one—to his own way; and the LORD has laid on him the iniquity of us all.

John 19:1-3, 6. Isaiah 53:5-6.

IT WAS THE THIRD HOUR
WHEN THEY CRUCIFIED [JESUS].

Those who passed by derided him, wagging their heads and saying, "Aha! You who would destroy the temple and rebuild it in three days, save yourself, and come down from the cross!"

So also the chief priests with the scribes mocked him to one another, saying, "He saved others; he cannot save himself. Let the Christ, the King of Israel, come down now from the cross that we may see and believe."

And at the ninth hour Jesus cried with a loud voice, "Eloi, Eloi, lema sabachthani?" which means, "My God, my God, why have you forsaken me?" And Jesus uttered a loud cry and breathed his last.

When the centurion, who stood facing him, saw that in this way he breathed his last, he said, "Truly this man was the Son of God!"

Mark 15:25, 29-32, 34, 37, 39.

"I AM THE ALPHA AND THE OMEGA,"
SAYS THE LORD GOD, "WHO IS AND WHO WAS AND
WHO IS TO COME, THE ALMIGHTY."

Now after the Sabbath, toward the dawn of the first day of the week, Mary Magdalene and the other Mary went to see the tomb. Behold, there was a great earthquake, for an angel of the Lord descended from heaven and . . . said to the women, "Do not be afraid, for I know that you seek Jesus who was crucified. He is not here, for he has risen, as he said. Come, see the place where he lay."

Christ died and lived again, that he might be Lord both of the dead and of the living.

Revelation 1:8. Matthew 28:1-2, 5-6. Romans 14:9.

O MY GOD, IN YOU I TRUST;
LET ME NOT BE PUT TO SHAME.

Make me to know your ways, O LORD; teach me your paths. Lead me in your truth and teach me, for you are the God of my salvation; for you I wait all the day long. Remember your mercy, O LORD, and your steadfast love, for they have been from of old. Remember not the sins of my youth or my transgressions; according to your steadfast love remember me, for the sake of your goodness, O LORD!

Good and upright is the LORD; therefore he instructs sinners in the way. He leads the humble in what is right, and teaches the humble his way. All the paths of the LORD are steadfast love and faithfulness, for those who keep his covenant and his testimonies.

Psalm 25:2, 4-10.

BEHOLD, GOD IS MY HELPER;
THE LORD IS THE UPHOLDER OF MY LIFE.

The LORD is on my side; I will not fear. What can man do to me?

The LORD is good, a stronghold in the day of trouble; he knows those who take refuge in him.

My flesh and my heart may fail, but God is the strength of my heart and my portion forever.

For me it is good to be near God; I have made the Lord GOD my refuge that I may tell of all *his* works.

Psalm 54:4. Psalm 118:6. Nahum 1:7. Psalm 73:26. Psalm 73:28.

WHO IS THERE TO HARM YOU IF YOU ARE ZEALOUS FOR WHAT IS GOOD?

But even if you should suffer for righteousness' sake, you will be blessed. Have no fear of them, nor be troubled, but in your hearts honor Christ the Lord as holy, always being prepared to make a defense to anyone who asks you for a reason for the hope that is in you; yet do it with gentleness and respect, having a good conscience, so that, when you are slandered, those who revile your good behavior in Christ may be put to shame.

For it is better to suffer for doing good, if that should be God's will, than for doing evil.

1 Peter 3:13-18.

> "Always being prepared to make a defense to anyone who asks you for a reason for the hope that is in you."

A WISE CHILD MAKES A GLAD FATHER.

Let no one despise you for your youth, but set the believers an example in speech, in conduct, in love, in faith, in purity.

Blessed are those whose way is blameless, who walk in the law of the LORD! Blessed are those who keep his testimonies, who seek him with their whole heart, who also do no wrong, but walk in his ways!

You have commanded your precepts to be kept diligently. Oh that my ways may be steadfast in keeping your statutes! Then I shall not be put to shame, having my eyes fixed on all your commandments.

I will praise you with an upright heart, when I learn your righteous rules. I will keep your statutes.

Proverbs 10:1. 1 Timothy 4:12. Psalm 119:1-8.

ALL THINGS ARE POSSIBLE FOR ONE
WHO BELIEVES.

Caleb quieted the people before Moses and said, "Let us go up at once and occupy it, for we are well able to overcome it." Then the men who had gone up with him said, "We are not able to go up against the people, for they are stronger than we are."

It is better to take refuge in the LORD than to trust in man.

When I am afraid, I put my trust in you. In God, whose word I praise, in God I trust; I shall not be afraid. What can flesh do to me?

Then my enemies will turn back in the day when I call. This I know, that God is for me.

Mark 9:23. Numbers 13:30-31. Psalm 118:8. Psalm 56:3-4, 9.

YOU GUIDE ME WITH YOUR COUNSEL, AND AFTERWARD YOU WILL RECEIVE ME TO GLORY.

No man has power to retain the spirit, or power over the day of death.

For we know that if the tent that is our earthly home is destroyed, we have a building from God, a house not made with hands, eternal in the heavens.

I [John] saw the holy city, new Jerusalem, coming down out of heaven from God, prepared as a bride adorned for her husband. And I heard a loud voice from the throne saying, "Behold, the dwelling place of God is with man. He will dwell with them, and they will be his people, and God himself will be with them as their God.

"He will wipe away every tear from their eyes, and death shall be no more, neither shall there be mourning, nor crying, nor pain anymore."

Psalm 73:24. Ecclesiastes 8:8. 2 Corinthians 5:1. Revelation 21:2-4.

COME, LORD JESUS!

Our citizenship is in heaven, and from it we await a Savior, the Lord Jesus Christ, who will transform our lowly body to be like his glorious body, by the power that enables him even to subject all things to himself.

People of old . . . all died in faith, not having received the things promised, but having seen them and greeted them from afar, and having acknowledged that they were strangers and exiles on the earth. For people who speak thus make it clear that they are seeking a homeland.

And so we will always be with the Lord.

Revelation 22:20. Philippians 3:20-21. Hebrews 11:2, 13-14. 1 Thessalonians 4:17.

GOD WILL BRING EVERY DEED INTO JUDGMENT, WITH EVERY SECRET THING, WHETHER GOOD OR EVIL.

The LORD sees not as man sees: man looks on the outward appearance, but the LORD looks on the heart.

Seek the LORD while he may be found; call upon him while he is near; let the wicked forsake his way, and the unrighteous man his thoughts; let him return to the LORD, that he may have compassion on him, and to our God, for he will abundantly pardon.

The LORD takes pleasure in those who fear him, in those who hope in his steadfast love.

Ecclesiastes 12:14. 1 Samuel 16:7. Isaiah 55:6-7. Psalm 147:11.

AM I A GOD AT HAND, DECLARES THE LORD, AND NOT A GOD FAR AWAY?

Can a man hide himself in secret places so that I cannot see him? declares the LORD. Do I not fill heaven and earth? declares the LORD.

O LORD, you have searched me and known me! You know when I sit down and when I rise up; you discern my thoughts from afar. You search out my path and my lying down and are acquainted with all my ways. Even before a word is on my tongue, behold, O LORD, you know it altogether.

No creature is hidden from his sight.

Jeremiah 23:23-24. Psalm 139:1-4. Hebrews 4:13.

MY EYES ARE ON ALL THEIR WAYS.
THEY ARE NOT HIDDEN FROM ME, NOR IS THEIR
INIQUITY CONCEALED FROM MY EYES.

Though you wash yourself with lye and use much soap, the stain of your guilt is still before me, declares the Lord GOD.

Remember not the sins of my youth or my transgressions. . . . For your name's sake, O LORD, pardon my guilt, for it is great. Consider my affliction and my trouble, and forgive all my sins.

I acknowledged my sin to you . . . and you forgave.

Blessed is the one whose transgression is forgiven, whose sin is covered.

Jeremiah 16:17. Jeremiah 2:22. Psalm 25:7, 11, 18. Psalm 32:5. Psalm 32:1.

IN THE BEGINNING WAS . . . [CHRIST].

All things were made through him, and without him was not any thing made that was made.

He was in the world, and the world was made through him, yet the world did not know him. He came to his own, and his own people did not receive him. But to all who did receive him, who believed in his name, he gave the right to become children of God.

See what kind of love the Father has given to us, that we should be called children of God; and so we are.

John 1:1, 3, 10-12. 1 John 3:1.

[THE LORD] SENT OUT HIS WORD
AND HEALED THEM.

When [Jesus] entered Capernaum, a centurion came forward to him, appealing to him, "Lord, my servant is lying paralyzed at home, suffering terribly."

[Jesus] said to him, "I will come and heal him."

But the centurion replied, "Lord, I am not worthy to have you come under my roof, but only say the word, and my servant will be healed."

When Jesus heard this, he marveled and said to those who followed him, "Truly, I tell you, with no one in Israel have I found such faith."

[God] is able to do far more abundantly than all that we ask or think.

Psalm 107:20. Matthew 8:5-8, 10. Ephesians 3:20.

[GOD] HAS MADE EVERYTHING BEAUTIFUL
IN ITS TIME.

In the beginning, God created the heavens and the earth. God said, "Let there be light," and there was light. And God saw that the light was good. And God separated the light from the darkness. God called the light Day, and the darkness he called Night.

God made the two great lights—the greater light to rule the day and the lesser light to rule the night—and the stars. And God set them in the expanse of the heavens to give light on the earth, to rule over the day and over the night, and to separate the light from the darkness.

Give thanks to the LORD . . . to him who made the great lights . . . the sun to rule over the day . . . the moon and stars to rule over the night, for his steadfast love endures forever.

Ecclesiastes 3:11. Genesis 1:1, 3-5, 16-18. Psalm 136:1, 7-9.

I WILL NEVER LEAVE YOU NOR FORSAKE YOU.

I will not leave you as orphans; I will come to you. I am with you always, to the end of the age. Fear not, I am the first and the last, and the living one. I died, and behold I am alive forevermore.

Who shall separate us from the love of Christ? . . . Neither death nor life, nor angels nor rulers, nor things present nor things to come, nor powers, nor height nor depth, nor anything else in all creation, will be able to separate us from the love of God in Christ Jesus our Lord.

So we can confidently say, "The Lord is my helper; I will not fear; what can man do to me?"

Hebrews 13:5. John 14:18. Matthew 28:20. Revelation 1:17-18. Romans 8:35, 38-39. Hebrews 13:6.

WONDROUSLY SHOW YOUR STEADFAST LOVE, O SAVIOR OF THOSE WHO SEEK REFUGE FROM THEIR ADVERSARIES AT YOUR RIGHT HAND.

Moses said to the people, "Fear not, stand firm, and see the salvation of the LORD, which he will work for you today. For the Egyptians whom you see today, you shall never see again. The LORD will fight for you, and you have only to be silent." Then Moses stretched out his hand over the sea, and the LORD drove the sea back by a strong east wind all night and made the sea dry land, and the waters were divided. And the people of Israel went into the midst of the sea on dry ground. . . . The Egyptians pursued and went in after them into the midst of the sea, all Pharaoh's horses, his chariots, and his horsemen.

Then the LORD said to Moses, "Stretch out your hand over the sea, that the water may come back upon the Egyptians, upon their chariots, and upon their horsemen." So Moses stretched out his hand over the sea, and the sea returned to its normal course when the morning appeared. Blessed be the LORD, for he has wondrously shown his steadfast love.

Psalm 17:7. Exodus 14:13-14, 21-23, 26-27. Psalm 31:21.

HEAVEN IS MY THRONE,
AND THE EARTH IS MY FOOTSTOOL.

All these things my hand has made, and so all these things came to be, declares the LORD.

Do you not know? Do you not hear? Has it not been told you from the beginning? Have you not understood from the foundations of the earth? It is he who sits above the circle of the earth, and its inhabitants are like grasshoppers; who stretches out the heavens like a curtain, and spreads them like a tent to dwell in.

To whom then will you compare me, that I should be like him? says the Holy One. Lift up your eyes on high and see: who created these? He who brings out their host by number, calling them all by name, by the greatness of his might, and because he is strong in power not one is missing.

Isaiah 66:1-2. Isaiah 40:21-22, 25-26.

"All these things my hand has made, and so all these things came to be, declares the LORD."

GIVE ME UNDERSTANDING,
THAT I MAY KNOW YOUR TESTIMONIES!

Your testimonies are wonderful; therefore my soul keeps them.

The unfolding of your words gives light; it imparts understanding to the simple.

Turn to me and be gracious to me, as is your way with those who love your name. Keep steady my steps according to your promise, and let no iniquity get dominion over me.

Righteous are you, O LORD, and right are your rules.

Your testimonies are righteous forever; give me understanding that I may live.

Psalm 119:125, 129-130, 132-133, 137, 144.

[GOD] IS WISE IN HEART AND MIGHTY IN
STRENGTH—WHO HAS HARDENED HIMSELF
AGAINST HIM, AND SUCCEEDED?

Behold, the fear of the Lord, that is wisdom, and to turn away from evil is understanding.

If he tears down, none can rebuild; if he shuts a man in, none can open. If he withholds the waters, they dry up; if he sends them out, they overwhelm the land.

Trust in the LORD with all your heart, and do not lean on your own understanding. In all your ways acknowledge him, and he will make straight your paths.

Behold, God is exalted in his power; who is a teacher like him?

Job 9:4. Job 28:28. Job 12:14-15. Proverbs 3:5-6. Job 36:22.

I WILL COME AGAIN.

The Lord is not slow to fulfill his promise as some count slowness, but is patient toward you, not wishing that any should perish, but that all should reach repentance.

But the day of the Lord will come like a thief, and then the heavens will pass away with a roar, and the heavenly bodies will be burned up and dissolved, and the earth and the works that are done on it will be exposed.

Since all these things are thus to be dissolved, what sort of people ought you to be in lives of holiness and godliness, waiting for and hastening the coming of the day of God . . . waiting for new heavens and a new earth in which righteousness dwells.

John 14:3. 2 Peter 3:9-13.

MAKE A JOYFUL NOISE TO THE LORD,
ALL THE EARTH; BREAK FORTH INTO JOYOUS SONG
AND SING PRAISES!

Sing praises to the LORD with the lyre, with the lyre and the sound of melody! With trumpets and the sound of the horn make a joyful noise before the King, the LORD!

Let the sea roar, and all that fills it; the world and those who dwell in it!

Let the rivers clap their hands; let the hills sing for joy together before the LORD, for he comes to judge the earth. He will judge the world with righteousness, and the peoples with equity.

Psalm 98:4-9.

LET YOUR MANNER OF LIFE BE WORTHY OF THE GOSPEL OF CHRIST.

Abstain from every form of evil.

If you are insulted for the name of Christ, you are blessed, because the Spirit of glory and of God rests upon you.

Do all things without grumbling or questioning, that you may be blameless and innocent, children of God without blemish in the midst of a crooked and twisted generation, among whom you shine as lights in the world.

Let not steadfast love and faithfulness forsake you; bind them around your neck; write them on the tablet of your heart. So you will find favor and good success in the sight of God and man.

Philippians 1:27. 1 Thessalonians 5:22. 1 Peter 4:14. Philippians 2:14-15. Proverbs 3:3-4.

JESUS SPOKE TO THEM, SAYING, "I AM THE LIGHT OF THE WORLD."

I have come into the world as light, so that whoever believes in me may not remain in darkness.

At one time you were darkness, but now you are light in the Lord. Walk as children of light (for the fruit of light is found in all that is good and right and true), and try to discern what is pleasing to the Lord.

Let us love one another, for love is from God, and whoever loves has been born of God and knows God. Anyone who does not love does not know God, because God is love.

John 8:12. John 12:46. Ephesians 5:8-10. 1 John 4:7-8.

WHOEVER LOVES DISCIPLINE LOVES KNOWLEDGE, BUT HE WHO HATES REPROOF IS STUPID.

The fear of the LORD is the beginning of knowledge; fools despise wisdom and instruction.

Hear . . . your father's instruction, and forsake not your mother's teaching, for they are a graceful garland for your head and pendants for your neck.

Continue in what you have learned and have firmly believed, knowing from whom you learned it and how from childhood you have been acquainted with the sacred writings, which are able to make you wise for salvation through faith in Christ Jesus.

Proverbs 12:1. Proverbs 1:7-9. 2 Timothy 3:14-15.

LET THE WORD OF CHRIST DWELL IN YOU RICHLY.

Blessed is the man who walks not in the counsel of the wicked, nor stands in the way of sinners, nor sits in the seat of scoffers; but his delight is in the law of the LORD, and on his law he meditates day and night.

As the rain and the snow come down from heaven and do not return there but water the earth, making it bring forth and sprout, giving seed to the sower and bread to the eater, so shall my word be that goes out from my mouth; it shall not return to me empty, but it shall accomplish that which I purpose.

All Scripture is breathed out by God and profitable for teaching, for reproof, for correction, and for training in righteousness, that the man of God may be competent, equipped for every good work.

Colossians 3:16. Psalm 1:1-2. Isaiah 55:10-11. 2 Timothy 3:16-17.

EXAMINE YOURSELVES, TO SEE WHETHER YOU ARE IN THE FAITH.

Whoever says "I know him" but does not keep his commandments is a liar, and the truth is not in him, but whoever keeps his word, in him truly the love of God is perfected. By this we may know that we are in him: whoever says he abides in him ought to walk in the same way in which he walked.

[Jesus] said, "Why do you call me 'Lord, Lord,' and not do what I tell you? Everyone who comes to me and hears my words and does them, I will show you what he is like: he is like a man building a house, who dug deep and laid the foundation on the rock. And when a flood arose, the stream broke against that house and could not shake it, because it had been well built.

"But the one who hears and does not do them is like a man who built a house on the ground without a foundation. When the stream broke against it, immediately it fell, and the ruin of that house was great."

2 Corinthians 13:5. 1 John 2:4-6. Luke 6:20, 46-49.

WHEN PRIDE COMES, THEN COMES DISGRACE.

Therefore let anyone who thinks that he stands take heed lest he fall.

There are those who curse their fathers and do not bless their mothers. There are those who are clean in their own eyes but are not washed of their filth.

A fool despises his father's instruction, but whoever heeds reproof is prudent.

A scoffer does not like to be reproved; he will not go to the wise.

The heart of him who has understanding seeks knowledge, but the mouths of fools feed on folly.

The ear that listens to life-giving reproof will dwell among the wise.

Proverbs 11:2. 1 Corinthians 10:12. Proverbs 30:11-12. Proverbs 15:5, 12, 14, 31.

WHATEVER YOU DO, IN WORD OR DEED,
DO EVERYTHING IN THE NAME OF THE LORD JESUS.

Do not be slothful in zeal, be fervent in spirit, serve the Lord.

The hand of the diligent will rule, while the slothful will be put to forced labor.

He who follows worthless pursuits lacks sense.

Besides that, they learn to be idlers, going about from house to house, and not only idlers, but also gossips and busybodies, saying what they should not.

Some among you walk in idleness, not busy at work, but busybodies. Now such persons we command and encourage in the Lord Jesus Christ to do their work quietly.

Whatever you do, work heartily, as for the Lord and not for men, knowing that from the Lord you will receive the inheritance as your reward. . . . For the wrongdoer will be paid back for the wrong he has done, and there is no partiality.

Colossians 3:17. Romans 12:11. Proverbs 12:24. Proverbs 12:11. 1 Timothy 5:13.
2 Thessalonians 3:11-12. Colossians 3:23-25.

THE LORD IS EXALTED, FOR HE DWELLS ON HIGH.

The LORD is high above all nations, and his glory above the heavens! Who is like the LORD our God, who is seated on high, who looks far down on the heavens and the earth?

He raises the poor from the dust and lifts the needy from the ash heap, to make them sit with princes, with the princes of his people.

Behold, the eye of the LORD is on those who fear him, on those who hope in his steadfast love.

The steadfast love of the LORD never ceases; his mercies never come to an end; they are new every morning; great is *his* faithfulness.

Isaiah 33:5. Psalm 113:4-8. Psalm 33:18. Lamentations 3:22-23.

GOD SHOWS HIS LOVE FOR US IN THAT WHILE WE WERE STILL SINNERS, CHRIST DIED FOR US.

Since, therefore, we have now been justified by his blood, much more shall we be saved by him from the wrath of God. For if while we were enemies we were reconciled to God by the death of his Son, much more, now that we are reconciled, shall we be saved by his life.

More than that, we also rejoice in God through our Lord Jesus Christ, through whom we have now received reconciliation.

We rejoice in hope of the glory of God.

Romans 5:8-11. Romans 5:2.

HEAR ... YOUR FATHER'S INSTRUCTION, AND FORSAKE NOT YOUR MOTHER'S TEACHING, FOR THEY ARE A GRACEFUL GARLAND FOR YOUR HEAD AND PENDANTS FOR YOUR NECK.

When I was a son with my father, tender, the only one in the sight of my mother, he taught me and said to me, "Let your heart hold fast my words; keep my commandments, and live.

"Get wisdom; get insight; do not forget, and do not turn away from the words of my mouth. Do not forsake her, and she will keep you; love her, and she will guard you.

"The beginning of wisdom is this: Get wisdom, and whatever you get, get insight. Prize her highly, and she will exalt you; she will honor you if you embrace her. She will place on your head a graceful garland; she will bestow on you a beautiful crown."

Proverbs 1:8-9. Proverbs 4:3-9.

O LORD, OUR LORD, HOW MAJESTIC IS YOUR NAME
IN ALL THE EARTH!

There is none holy like the LORD; there is none besides you; there is no rock like our God.

For you are great and do wondrous things; you alone are God.

You are the God, you alone, of all the kingdoms of the earth; you have made heaven and earth.

Yours, O LORD, is the greatness and the power and the glory and the victory and the majesty, for all that is in the heavens and in the earth is yours. Yours is the kingdom, O LORD, and you are exalted as head above all. Both riches and honor come from you, and you rule over all. In your hand are power and might, and in your hand it is to make great and to give strength to all.

Psalm 8:1. 1 Samuel 2:2. Psalm 86:10. 2 Kings 19:15. 1 Chronicles 29:11-12.

BRING ME BACK THAT I MAY BE RESTORED,
FOR YOU ARE THE LORD MY GOD.

After I had turned away, I relented, and after I was instructed, I struck my thigh; I was ashamed, and I was confounded, because I bore the disgrace of my youth.

The LORD waits to be gracious to you, and therefore he exalts himself to show mercy to you. For the LORD is a God of justice; blessed are all those who wait for him.

Your ears shall hear a word behind you, saying, "This is the way, walk in it," when you turn to the right or when you turn to the left.

Bless our God, O peoples; let the sound of his praise be heard, who has kept our soul among the living and has not let our feet slip.

Jeremiah 31:18-19. Isaiah 30:18, 21. Psalm 66:8-9.

ALL THINGS COME FROM YOU,
AND OF YOUR OWN HAVE WE GIVEN YOU.

There is nothing better for a person than that he should eat and drink and find enjoyment in his toil. This also, I saw, is from the hand of God, for apart from him who can eat or who can have enjoyment? For to the one who pleases him God has given wisdom and knowledge and joy.

From your lofty abode you water the mountains; the earth is satisfied with the fruit of your work. You cause the grass to grow for the livestock and plants [to grow] for man to cultivate.

You give food to all flesh, for *your* steadfast love endures forever.

1 Chronicles 29:14. Ecclesiastes 2:24-26. Psalm 104:13-14. Psalm 136:25.

LET US COME INTO HIS PRESENCE WITH
THANKSGIVING; LET US MAKE A JOYFUL NOISE
TO HIM WITH SONGS OF PRAISE!

It is good to give thanks to the LORD, to sing praises to your name, O Most High; to declare your steadfast love in the morning, and your faithfulness by night, to the music of the lute and the harp, to the melody of the lyre.

For the LORD is a great God, and a great King above all gods. In his hand are the depths of the earth; the heights of the mountains are his also. The sea is his, for he made it, and his hands formed the dry land.

Oh come, let us worship and bow down; let us kneel before the LORD, our Maker! For he is our God, and we are the people of his pasture, and the sheep of his hand.

Psalm 95:2. Psalm 92:1-3. Psalm 95:3-7.

BY FAITH THE WALLS OF JERICHO FELL DOWN AFTER THEY HAD BEEN ENCIRCLED FOR SEVEN DAYS.

The LORD said to Joshua, "See, I have given Jericho into your hand, with its king and mighty men of valor. You shall march around the city, all the men of war going around the city once. Thus shall you do for six days. . . . On the seventh day you shall march around the city seven times, and the priests shall blow the trumpets. And when they make a long blast with the ram's horn, when you hear the sound of the trumpet, then all the people shall shout with a great shout, and the wall of the city will fall down flat."

The king is not saved by his great army; a warrior is not delivered by his great strength.

Clap your hands, all peoples! Shout to God with loud songs of joy! He subdued peoples under us, and nations under our feet. God has gone up with a shout, the LORD with the sound of a trumpet. Sing praises to God, sing praises! . . . For God is the King of all the earth.

Hebrews 11:30. Joshua 6:2-5. Psalm 33:16. Psalm 47:1, 3, 5-7.

TEACH ME YOUR WAY, O LORD.

What does the LORD your God require of you, but to fear the LORD your God, to walk in all his ways, to love him, to serve the LORD your God with all your heart and with all your soul, and to keep the commandments and statutes of the LORD, which I am commanding you today for your good?

Learn them and be careful to do them.

That will be your wisdom and your understanding.

Only take care, and keep your soul diligently, lest you forget the things that your eyes have seen, and lest they depart from your heart all the days of your life.

Psalm 27:11. Deuteronomy 10:12-13. Deuteronomy 5:1. Deuteronomy 4:6, 9.

WISDOM IS BETTER THAN JEWELS.

Blessed is the one who finds wisdom, and the one who gets understanding, for the gain from her is better than gain from silver and her profit better than gold.

She is more precious than jewels, and nothing you desire can compare with her. Long life is in her right hand; in her left hand are riches and honor. Her ways are ways of pleasantness, and all her paths are peace.

She is a tree of life to those who lay hold of her; those who hold her fast are called blessed.

Proverbs 8:11. Proverbs 3:13-18.

PURSUE LOVE.

If I speak in the tongues of men and of angels, but have not love, I am a noisy gong or a clanging cymbal. If I give away all I have . . . but have not love, I gain nothing.

Love is patient and kind; love does not envy or boast; it is not arrogant or rude. It does not insist on its own way; it is not irritable or resentful; it does not rejoice at wrongdoing, but rejoices with the truth. Love bears all things, believes all things, hopes all things, endures all things.

A friend loves at all times.

1 Corinthians 14:1. 1 Corinthians 13:1, 3-7. Proverbs 17:17.

THE WAY OF THE WICKED IS AN ABOMINATION TO THE LORD, BUT HE LOVES HIM WHO PURSUES RIGHTEOUSNESS.

"Behold, I will press you down in your place, as a cart full of sheaves presses down. Flight shall perish from the swift, and the strong shall not retain his strength, nor shall the mighty save his life; he who handles the bow shall not stand, and he who is swift of foot shall not save himself, nor shall he who rides the horse save his life; and he who is stout of heart among the mighty shall flee away naked in that day," declares the LORD.

Note then the kindness and the severity of God: severity toward those who have fallen, but God's kindness to you, provided you continue in his kindness.

Proverbs 15:9. Amos 2:13-16. Romans 11:22.

THE LORD HAS TAKEN HIS PLACE TO CONTEND; HE STANDS TO JUDGE PEOPLES.

It is God who executes judgment, putting down one and lifting up another.

If you, O LORD, should mark iniquities, O Lord, who could stand? But with you there is forgiveness, that you may be feared.

He does not deal with us according to our sins, nor repay us according to our iniquities. For as high as the heavens are above the earth, so great is his steadfast love toward those who fear him; as far as the east is from the west, so far does he remove our transgressions from us.

He knows our frame; he remembers that we are dust.

Isaiah 3:13. Psalm 75:7. Psalm 130:3-4. Psalm 103:10-12, 14.

THE IDOLS OF THE NATIONS ARE SILVER AND GOLD, THE WORK OF HUMAN HANDS.

A tree from the forest is cut down and worked with an axe by the hands of a craftsman. They decorate it with silver and gold; they fasten it with hammer and nails so that it cannot move.

Their idols are like scarecrows in a cucumber field, and they cannot speak; they have to be carried, for they cannot walk. Do not be afraid of them, for they cannot do evil, neither is it in them to do good.

All the gods of the peoples are worthless idols, but the LORD made the heavens.

There is none like you, O LORD; you are great, and your name is great in might. Who would not fear you, O King of the nations? For this is your due; for among all the wise ones of the nations and in all their kingdoms there is none like you.

Psalm 135:15. Jeremiah 10:3-5. Psalm 96:5. Jeremiah 10:6-7.

OH COME, LET US SING TO THE LORD; LET US MAKE A JOYFUL NOISE TO THE ROCK OF OUR SALVATION!

They sing the song of Moses, the servant of God, and the song of the Lamb, saying,

"Great and amazing are your deeds,
O Lord God the Almighty!
Just and true are your ways,
O King of the nations!
Who will not fear, O Lord,
and glorify your name?
For you alone are holy.
All nations will come
and worship you,
for your righteous acts have been revealed."

Psalm 95:1. Revelation 15:3-4.

HOLY, HOLY, HOLY IS THE LORD OF HOSTS; THE WHOLE EARTH IS FULL OF HIS GLORY!

He loves righteousness and justice; the earth is full of the steadfast love of the LORD.

Who is like you, O LORD, among the gods? Who is like you, majestic in holiness, awesome in glorious deeds, doing wonders? You have led in your steadfast love the people whom you have redeemed.

As he who called you is holy, you also be holy in all your conduct, since it is written, "You shall be holy, for I am holy."

Be diligent to be found by him without spot or blemish, and at peace.

Isaiah 6:3. Psalm 33:5. Exodus 15:11, 13. 1 Peter 1:15-16. 2 Peter 3:14.

DO NOT BE DECEIVED.

God is not mocked, for whatever one sows, that will he also reap. For the one who sows to his own flesh will from the flesh reap corruption, but the one who sows to the Spirit will from the Spirit reap eternal life. And let us not grow weary of doing good, for in due season we will reap, if we do not give up.

For what will it profit a man if he gains the whole world and forfeits his soul? Or what shall a man give in return for his soul? For the Son of Man is going to come with his angels in the glory of his Father, and then he will repay each person according to what he has done.

Galatians 6:7-9. Matthew 16:26-27.

DO NOT BE CONFORMED TO THIS WORLD.

Do not be unequally yoked with unbelievers. For what partnership has righteousness with lawlessness? Or what fellowship has light with darkness? What accord has Christ with Belial? Or what portion does a believer share with an unbeliever? What agreement has the temple of God with idols? For we are the temple of the living God; as God said, "I will make my dwelling among them and walk among them, and I will be their God, and they shall be my people."

Do not love the world or the things in the world. If anyone loves the world, the love of the Father is not in him. The world is passing away along with its desires, but whoever does the will of God abides forever.

Romans 12:2. 2 Corinthians 6:14-16. 1 John 2:15, 17.

WHATEVER YOUR HAND FINDS TO DO,
DO IT WITH YOUR MIGHT.

Go to the ant . . . consider her ways, and be wise. Without having any chief, officer, or ruler, she prepares her bread in summer and gathers her food in harvest.

Love not sleep, lest you come to poverty; open your eyes, and you will have plenty of bread.

Aspire to live quietly, and to mind your own affairs, and to work with your hands.

As we have opportunity, let us do good to everyone, and especially to those who are of the household of faith.

Ecclesiastes 9:10. Proverbs 6:6-8. Proverbs 20:13. 1 Thessalonians 4:11.
Galatians 6:10.

LET YOUR LIGHT SHINE.

Do not neglect to do good and to share what you have, for such sacrifices are pleasing to God.

If your enemy is hungry, give him bread to eat, and if he is thirsty, give him water to drink,

Then shall your light break forth like the dawn, and your healing shall spring up speedily; your righteousness shall go before you; the glory of the LORD shall be your rear guard.

You are the light of the world. A city set on a hill cannot be hidden. Nor do people light a lamp and put it under a basket, but on a stand, and it gives light to all in the house. In the same way, let your light shine before others, so that they may see your good works and give glory to your Father who is in heaven.

Matthew 5:16. Hebrews 13:16. Proverbs 25:21. Isaiah 58:8. Matthew 5:14-16.

"Let us do good to everyone, and especially to those who are of the household of faith."

BEHOLD, HOW GOOD AND PLEASANT IT IS
WHEN BROTHERS DWELL IN UNITY!

Let love be genuine. Abhor what is evil; hold fast to what is good. Love one another with brotherly affection. Outdo one another in showing honor.

Do nothing from rivalry or conceit, but in humility count others more significant than yourselves.

The meek shall inherit the land and delight themselves in abundant peace.

And it is my prayer that your love may abound more and more, with knowledge and all discernment . . . be pure and blameless . . . filled with the fruit of righteousness that comes through Jesus Christ, to the glory and praise of God.

Psalm 133:1. Romans 12:9-10. Philippians 2:3. Psalm 37:11. Philippians 1:9-11.

LOVE IS FROM GOD.

Ruth clung to [Naomi]. And [Naomi] said, "See, your sister-in-law has gone back to her people and to her gods; return after your sister-in-law." But Ruth said, "Do not urge me to leave you or to return from following you. For where you go I will go, and where you lodge I will lodge. Your people shall be my people, and your God my God. Where you die I will die, and there will I be buried."

A friend loves at all times, and a brother is born for adversity.

Anyone who does not love does not know God, because God is love. In this is love, not that we have loved God but that he loved us. . . . If God so loved us, we also ought to love one another. . . . If we love one another, God abides in us and his love is perfected in us.

1 John 4:7. Ruth 1:14-17. Proverbs 17:17. 1 John 4:8, 10-12.

GOD SO LOVED THE WORLD.

He who did not spare his own Son but gave him up for us all, how will he not also with him graciously give us all things?

God so loved the world, that he gave his only Son, that whoever believes in him should not perish but have eternal life.

Who is to condemn? Christ Jesus is the one who died—more than that, who was raised—who is at the right hand of God, who indeed is interceding for us. Neither death nor life, nor angels nor rulers, nor things present nor things to come, nor powers, nor height nor depth, nor anything else in all creation, will be able to separate us from the love of God in Christ Jesus our Lord.

John 3:16. Romans 8:32. John 3:16. Romans 8:34, 38-39.

I WILL TELL WHAT HE HAS DONE FOR MY SOUL.

My mouth will tell of your righteous acts, of your deeds of salvation all the day, for their number is past my knowledge.

Let your steadfast love come to me, O LORD, your salvation according to your promise; then shall I have an answer for him who taunts me, for I trust in your word.

I will keep your law continually, forever and ever, and I shall walk in a wide place, for I have sought your precepts.

Psalm 66:16. Psalm 71:15. Psalm 119:41-42, 44-45.

THE MOST HIGH . . . DOES ACCORDING TO HIS WILL.

Commit your way to the LORD; trust in him, and he will act.

Do not be anxious about anything, but in everything by prayer and supplication with thanksgiving let your requests be made known to God.

Humble yourselves, therefore, under the mighty hand of God so that at the proper time he may exalt you, casting all your anxieties on him, because he cares for you.

Delight yourself in the LORD, and he will give you the desires of your heart.

Daniel 4:34-35. Psalm 37:5. Philippians 4:6. 1 Peter 5:6-7. Psalm 37:4.

IN THE PATH OF RIGHTEOUSNESS IS LIFE.

While bodily training is of some value, godliness is of value in every way, as it holds promise for the present life and also for the life to come.

Blessed are they who observe justice, who do righteousness at all times!

For the kingdom of God is not a matter of eating and drinking but of righteousness and peace and joy in the Holy Spirit. Whoever thus serves Christ is acceptable to God and approved by men. So then let us pursue what makes for peace and for mutual upbuilding.

Better is a dry morsel with quiet than a house full of feasting with strife.

Proverbs 12:28. 1 Timothy 4:8. Psalm 106:3. Romans 14:17-19. Proverbs 17:1.

A WISE MAN'S HEART INCLINES HIM TO THE RIGHT.

Look carefully then how you walk, not as unwise but as wise, making the best use of the time, because the days are evil. Therefore do not be foolish, but understand what the will of the Lord is.

Walk in wisdom toward outsiders, making the best use of the time. Let your speech always be gracious, seasoned with salt, so that you may know how you ought to answer each person.

Show yourself in all respects to be a model of good works.

Ecclesiastes 10:2. Ephesians 5:15-17. Colossians 4:5-6. Titus 2:7.

A FOOL'S LIPS WALK INTO A FIGHT, AND HIS MOUTH INVITES A BEATING.

It is an honor for a man to keep aloof from strife, but every fool will be quarreling.

Drive out a scoffer, and strife will go out, and quarreling and abuse will cease.

Finally, all of you, have unity of mind, sympathy, brotherly love, a tender heart, and a humble mind. Do not repay evil for evil or reviling for reviling, but on the contrary, bless.

Walk in a manner worthy of the calling to which you have been called, with all humility and gentleness, with patience, bearing with one another in love, eager to maintain the unity of the Spirit in the bond of peace.

He who loves purity of heart, and whose speech is gracious, will have the king as his friend.

Proverbs 18:6. Proverbs 20:3. Proverbs 22:10. 1 Peter 3:8-9. Ephesians 4:1-3. Proverbs 22:11.

WHATEVER OVERCOMES A PERSON, TO THAT HE IS ENSLAVED.

Cain was very angry, and his face fell. The LORD said to Cain, "Why are you angry, and why has your face fallen? If you do well, will you not be accepted? And if you do not do well, sin is crouching at the door. Its desire is for you, but you must rule over it."

You must put them all away: anger, wrath, malice, slander, and obscene talk from your mouth.

Let every person be quick to hear, slow to speak, slow to anger; for the anger of man does not produce the righteousness of God.

Be doers of the word, and not hearers only.

2 Peter 2:19. Genesis 4:5-7. Colossians 3:8. James 1:19-20, 22.

AS A FATHER SHOWS COMPASSION TO HIS CHILDREN, SO THE LORD SHOWS COMPASSION TO THOSE WHO FEAR HIM.

In Christ Jesus you are all *children* of God, through faith.

For all who are led by the Spirit of God are *children* of God.

See what kind of love the Father has given to us, that we should be called children of God; and so we are.

I [God] will betroth you to me forever. I will betroth you to me in righteousness and in justice, in steadfast love and in mercy.

The LORD is good, a stronghold in the day of trouble.

Psalm 103:13. Galatians 3:26. Romans 8:14. 1 John 3:1. Hosea 2:19. Nahum 1:7.

I KNOW THE PLANS I HAVE FOR YOU, DECLARES THE LORD.

He [God] predestined us for adoption as *children* through Jesus Christ, according to the purpose of his will.

He saved us and called us to a holy calling, not because of our works but because of his own purpose and grace, which he gave us in Christ Jesus before the ages began.

You did not choose me, but I chose you and appointed you that you should go and bear fruit and that your fruit should abide, so that whatever you ask the Father in my name, he may give it to you.

The fruit of the Spirit is love, joy, peace, patience, kindness, goodness, faithfulness, gentleness, self-control; against such things there is no law.

Jeremiah 29:11. Ephesians 1:5. 2 Timothy 1:9. John 15:16. Galatians 5:22-23.

THE TEMPTER CAME AND SAID TO [JESUS]—

—"If you are the Son of God, command these stones to become loaves of bread. . . . Throw yourself down, for it is written, 'He will command his angels concerning you.'" The devil . . . showed him all the kingdoms of the world. . . . "All these I will give you, if you will fall down and worship me."

Then Jesus said to him, "Be gone, Satan! For it is written, 'You shall worship the Lord your God and him only shall you serve.'"

Beloved, do not be surprised at the fiery trial when it comes upon you to test you, as though something strange were happening to you. But rejoice insofar as you share Christ's sufferings, that you may also rejoice and be glad when his glory is revealed.

Be sober-minded; be watchful. Your adversary the devil prowls around like a roaring lion, seeking someone to devour.

Submit yourselves therefore to God. Resist the devil, and he will flee from you.

Matthew 4:3, 6, 8-10. 1 Peter 4:12-13. 1 Peter 5:8. James 4:7.

WALK IN THE WAY OF THE GOOD AND KEEP TO THE PATHS OF THE RIGHTEOUS.

Keep sound wisdom and discretion, and they will be life for your soul and adornment for your neck.

Then you will walk on your way securely, and your foot will not stumble. If you lie down, you will not be afraid; when you lie down, your sleep will be sweet.

Do not be afraid of sudden terror or of the ruin of the wicked, when it comes, for the LORD will be your confidence and will keep your foot from being caught.

Do not withhold good from those to whom it is due, when it is in your power to do it. Do not say to your neighbor, "Go, and come again, tomorrow I will give it"—when you have it with you.

Proverbs 2:20. Proverbs 3:21-28.

"Walk in the way of the good and keep to the paths of the righteous."

IF ANYONE IS IN CHRIST, HE IS A NEW CREATION.

Thus says the Lord GOD . . . "I will sprinkle clean water on you, and you shall be clean from all your uncleannesses, and from all your idols I will cleanse you. And I will give you a new heart, and a new spirit I will put within you. And I will remove the heart of stone from your flesh and give you a heart of flesh. And I will put my Spirit within you, and cause you to walk in my statutes and be careful to obey my rules."

God, being rich in mercy, because of the great love with which he loved us, even when we were dead in our trespasses, made us alive together with Christ. . . . By grace you have been saved through faith. And this is not your own doing; it is the gift of God, not a result of works, so that no one may boast.

For we are his workmanship, created in Christ Jesus for good works, which God prepared beforehand, that we should walk in them.

2 Corinthians 5:17. Ezekiel 36:22, 25-27. Ephesians 2:4-5, 8-10.

"ALL PEOPLE WILL KNOW THAT YOU ARE MY DISCIPLES IF YOU HAVE LOVE FOR ONE ANOTHER."

Let all that you do be done in love.

Put on then, as God's chosen ones, holy and beloved, compassionate hearts, kindness, humility, meekness, and patience, bearing with one another and, if one has a complaint against another, forgiving each other; as the Lord has forgiven you, so you also must forgive. And above all these put on love, which binds everything together in perfect harmony.

May the God of endurance and encouragement grant you to live in such harmony with one another.

John 13:35. 1 Corinthians 16:14. Colossians 3:12-14. Romans 15:5.

THE LORD IS GRACIOUS AND MERCIFUL.

The LORD is good to all, and his mercy is over all that he has made.

He has told you, O man, what is good; and what does the LORD require of you but to do justice, and to love kindness, and to walk humbly with your God?

Let not steadfast love and faithfulness forsake you; bind them around your neck; write them on the tablet of your heart.

Whoever pursues righteousness and kindness will find life, righteousness, and honor.

Love your enemies and pray for those who persecute you, so that you may be *children* of your Father who is in heaven.

Be merciful, even as your Father is merciful.

Psalm 145:8. Psalm 145:9. Micah 6:8. Proverbs 3:3. Proverbs 21:21.
Matthew 5:44-45. Luke 6:36.

KEEP THE COMMANDMENTS OF THE LORD
YOUR GOD AND WALK IN HIS WAYS.

Jesus said, "The one who walks in the darkness does not know where he is going."

"I am the light of the world. Whoever follows me will not walk in darkness, but will have the light of life."

Now that you have been set free from sin and have become slaves of God, the fruit you get leads to sanctification and its end, eternal life.

As he who called you is holy, you also be holy in all your conduct, since it is written, "You shall be holy, for I am holy."

If we live by the Spirit, let us also walk by the Spirit.

Deuteronomy 28:9. John 12:35. John 8:12. Romans 6:22. 1 Peter 1:15-16.
Galatians 5:25.

I WILL PONDER THE WAY THAT IS BLAMELESS. . . .

. . . I will walk with integrity of heart within my house.

But I see . . . another law waging war against the law of my mind and making me captive to the law of sin.

Turn away the reproach that I dread, for your rules are good. Behold, I long for your precepts; in your righteousness give me life!

Let your steadfast love come to me, O LORD, your salvation according to your promise; then shall I have an answer for him who taunts me, for I trust in your word. And take not the word of truth utterly out of my mouth, for my hope is in your rules.

I will keep your law continually, forever and ever, and I shall walk in a wide place, for I have sought your precepts. I find my delight in your commandments, which I love.

Psalm 101:2. Romans 7:23. Psalm 119:39-45, 47.

WHOEVER IS WISE,
LET HIM UNDERSTAND THESE THINGS.

Blessed are the poor in spirit, for theirs is the kingdom of heaven. ✧ O God, you know my folly; the wrongs I have done are not hidden from you.

Blessed are those who mourn, for they shall be comforted. ✧ I confess my iniquity; I am sorry for my sin.

Blessed are the meek, for they shall inherit the earth. ✧ Humble yourselves before the Lord, and he will exalt you.

Blessed are those who hunger and thirst for righteousness, for they shall be satisfied. ✧ Then you will understand righteousness and justice and equity, every good path; for wisdom will come into your heart, and knowledge will be pleasant to your soul.

Hosea 14:9. Matthew 5:3. Psalm 69:5. Matthew 5:4. Psalm 38:18. Matthew 5:5. James 4:10. Matthew 5:6. Proverbs 2:9-10.

THE WAYS OF THE LORD ARE RIGHT, AND THE UPRIGHT WALK IN THEM.

Blessed are the merciful, for they shall receive mercy. ✧ It is more blessed to give than to receive. ✧ Be kind to one another, tenderhearted, forgiving one another.

Blessed are the pure in heart, for they shall see God. ✧ He who has clean hands and a pure heart, who does not lift up his soul to what is false and does not swear deceitfully . . . will receive blessing from the LORD and righteousness from the God of his salvation.

Blessed are the peacemakers, for they shall be called sons of God. ✧ Deceit is in the heart of those who devise evil, but those who plan peace have joy.

Hosea 14:9. Matthew 5:7. Acts 20:35. Ephesians 4:32. Matthew 5:8. Psalm 24:4-5. Matthew 5:9. Proverbs 12:20.

DO NOT REBUKE AN OLDER MAN . . . [TREAT] OLDER WOMEN AS MOTHERS.

The years of our life are seventy, or even by reason of strength eighty; yet their span is but toil and trouble; they are soon gone, and we fly away.

Bear one another's burdens, and so fulfill the law of Christ. And let us not grow weary of doing good. . . . As we have opportunity, let us do good to everyone, and especially to those who are of the household of faith.

Young men and maidens together, old men and children! Let them praise the name of the LORD, for his name alone is exalted; his majesty is above earth and heaven.

1 Timothy 5:1-2. Psalm 90:10. Galatians 6:2, 9-10. Psalm 148:12-13.

THE LORD REIGNS.

He is robed in majesty; the LORD is robed; he has put on strength as his belt. Yes, the world is established; it shall never be moved.

Your throne is established from of old; you are from everlasting.

The floods have lifted up, O LORD, the floods have lifted up their voice; the floods lift up their roaring. Mightier than the thunders of many waters, mightier than the waves of the sea, the LORD on high is mighty!

Your decrees are very trustworthy; holiness befits your house, O LORD, forevermore.

Psalm 93:1-5.

TO WHOM THEN WILL YOU LIKEN GOD?

It is he who sits above the circle of the earth, and its inhabitants are like grasshoppers; who stretches out the heavens like a curtain, and spreads them like a tent to dwell in; who brings princes to nothing, and makes the rulers of the earth as emptiness.

Scarcely are they planted, scarcely sown, scarcely has their stem taken root in the earth, when he blows on them, and they wither, and the tempest carries them off like stubble.

To whom then will you compare me, that I should be like him? says the Holy One. Lift up your eyes on high and see: who created these? He who brings out their host by number, calling them all by name, by the greatness of his might, and because he is strong in power not one is missing.

Great is our Lord, and abundant in power.

Isaiah 40:18, 22-26. Psalm 147:5.

WITH GOD ARE WISDOM AND MIGHT; HE HAS COUNSEL AND UNDERSTANDING.

I have taught you the way of wisdom; I have led you in the paths of uprightness. When you walk, your step will not be hampered, and if you run, you will not stumble. Keep hold of instruction; do not let go; guard her, for she is your life.

Be attentive to my words; incline your ear to my sayings. Let them not escape from your sight; keep them within your heart.

You shall love the LORD your God with all your heart and with all your soul and with all your might.

Job 12:13. Proverbs 4:11-13, 20-21. Deuteronomy 6:5.

COME, O CHILDREN, LISTEN TO ME; I WILL TEACH YOU THE FEAR OF THE LORD.

What man is there who desires life and loves many days, that he may see good?

Keep your tongue from evil and your lips from speaking deceit. Turn away from evil and do good; seek peace and pursue it. The eyes of the LORD are toward the righteous and his ears toward their cry.

The face of the LORD is against those who do evil, to cut off the memory of them from the earth.

When the righteous cry for help, the LORD hears and delivers them out of all their troubles.

Psalm 34:11-17.

EVERY FOOL WILL BE QUARRELING.

Pride goes before destruction, and a haughty spirit before a fall.

What causes quarrels and what causes fights among you?

If you have bitter jealousy and selfish ambition in your hearts . . . this is not the wisdom that comes down from above. . . . For where jealousy and selfish ambition exist, there will be disorder and every vile practice.

Cast off the works of darkness and put on the armor of light. Let us walk properly . . . not in quarreling and jealousy.

In all these things we are more than conquerors through [Christ] who loved us.

Proverbs 20:3. Proverbs 16:18. James 4:1. James 3:14-16. Romans 13:12-13. Romans 8:37.

WE MUST PAY MUCH CLOSER ATTENTION TO WHAT WE HAVE HEARD, LEST WE DRIFT AWAY FROM IT.

See, I have taught you statutes and rules. . . . Keep them and do them, for that will be your wisdom and your understanding.

Only take care, and keep your soul diligently, lest you forget the things that your eyes have seen, and lest they depart from your heart all the days of your life.

Seek the LORD your God and you will find him, if you search after him with all your heart and with all your soul. For the LORD your God is a merciful God. He will not leave you.

Be watchful, stand firm in the faith . . . be strong.

Hebrews 2:1. Deuteronomy 4:5-6, 9, 29, 31. 1 Corinthians 16:13.

DOES NOT WISDOM CALL?

Learn prudence . . . learn sense. Hear, for I will speak noble things, and from my lips will come what is right. I have counsel and sound wisdom; I have insight; I have strength. By me kings reign, and rulers decree what is just; by me princes rule, and nobles, all who govern justly.

Riches and honor are with me, enduring wealth and righteousness. My fruit is better than gold, even fine gold, and my yield than choice silver.

I walk in the way of righteousness, in the paths of justice, granting an inheritance to those who love me, and filling their treasuries.

Proverbs 8:1, 5-6, 14-16, 18-21.

THE SEVENTH DAY IS A SABBATH TO THE LORD YOUR GOD.

If you turn back your foot from the Sabbath, from doing your pleasure on my holy day, and call the Sabbath a delight and the holy day of the LORD honorable; if you honor it, not going your own ways, or seeking your own pleasure, or talking idly; then you shall take delight in the LORD, and I will make you ride on the heights of the earth; I will feed you with the heritage of Jacob your father, for the mouth of the LORD has spoken.

Let us consider how to stir up one another to love and good works, not neglecting to meet together, as is the habit of some, but encouraging one another, and all the more as you see the Day drawing near.

Exodus 20:10. Isaiah 58:13-14. Hebrews 10:24-25.

WE ARE WAITING FOR NEW HEAVENS AND A
NEW EARTH IN WHICH RIGHTEOUSNESS DWELLS.

I know that my Redeemer lives, and at the last he will stand upon the earth.

Now we see [God] in a mirror dimly, but then face to face. Now I know [him] in part; then I shall know fully.

He will wipe away every tear from their eyes, and death shall be no more, neither shall there be mourning, nor crying, nor pain anymore.

No eye has seen, nor ear heard, nor the heart of man imagined, what God has prepared for those who love him.

2 Peter 3:13. Job 19:25. 1 Corinthians 13:12. Revelation 21:4. 1 Corinthians 2:9.

"No eye has seen, nor ear heard, nor the heart of man imagined, what God has prepared for those who love him."

THE LORD IS MY ROCK AND MY FORTRESS
AND MY DELIVERER.

For he will hide me in his shelter in the day of trouble; he will conceal me under the cover of his tent; he will lift me high upon a rock.

In you, O LORD, do I take refuge; let me never be put to shame; in your righteousness deliver me! Incline your ear to me; rescue me speedily! Be a rock of refuge for me, a strong fortress to save me!

Oh, taste and see that the LORD is good! Blessed is the man who takes refuge in him! Oh, fear the LORD, you his saints, for those who fear him have no lack! The young lions suffer want and hunger; but those who seek the LORD lack no good thing.

2 Samuel 22:2. Psalm 27:5. Psalm 31:1-2. Psalm 34:8-10.

BLESS THE LORD.

Bless the LORD, O my soul, and forget not all his benefits, who forgives all your iniquity, who heals all your diseases, who redeems your life from the pit, who crowns you with steadfast love and mercy, who satisfies you with good so that your youth is renewed like the eagle's.

What then shall we say to these things? If God is for us, who can be against us? He who did not spare his own Son but gave him up for us all, how will he not also with him graciously give us all things?

God will supply every need of yours according to his riches in glory in Christ Jesus. To our God and Father be glory forever and ever. Amen.

Psalm 103:1-5. Romans 8:31-32. Philippians 4:19-20.

[GOD'S] WORDS WILL NOT PASS AWAY.

The grass withers, the flower fades, but the word of our God will stand forever.

Incline your ear, and hear the words of the wise, and apply your heart to my knowledge, for it will be pleasant if you keep them within you, if all of them are ready on your lips.

For the word of God is living and active.

When I think of your rules from of old, I take comfort, O Lord. I promise to keep your words. I entreat your favor with all my heart; be gracious to me according to your promise. Righteous are you, O Lord, and right are your rules.

Luke 21:33. Isaiah 40:8. Proverbs 22:17-18. Hebrews 4:12. Psalm 119:52, 57-58, 137.

PRAY THEN LIKE THIS.

Our Father in heaven, hallowed be your name.

Your kingdom come, your will be done, on earth as it is in heaven.

Give us this day our daily bread, and forgive us our debts, as we also have forgiven our debtors.

And lead us not into temptation, but deliver us from evil.

When you pray, do not heap up empty phrases as the Gentiles do, for they think that they will be heard for their many words. Do not be like them, for your Father knows what you need before you ask him.

Matthew 6:9-13. Matthew 6:7-8.

PUT ON THE WHOLE ARMOR OF GOD.

We do not wrestle against flesh and blood, but against the rulers, against the authorities, against the cosmic powers over this present darkness, against the spiritual forces of evil in the heavenly places. Therefore take up the whole armor of God, that you may be able to withstand in the evil day, and having done all, to stand firm.

In all circumstances take up the shield of faith . . . the helmet of salvation, and the sword of the Spirit, which is the word of God, praying at all times in the Spirit, with all prayer and supplication.

Ephesians 6:11-13, 16-18.

DO YOU NOT KNOW THAT IN A RACE ALL THE RUNNERS RUN, BUT ONLY ONE RECEIVES THE PRIZE? SO RUN THAT YOU MAY OBTAIN IT.

Every athlete exercises self-control in all things. They do it to receive a perishable wreath, but we an imperishable.

Let us run with endurance the race that is set before us, looking to Jesus, the founder and perfecter of our faith, who for the joy that was set before him endured the cross, despising the shame, and is seated at the right hand of the throne of God.

Pursue righteousness, godliness, faith, love, steadfastness, gentleness.

He who began a good work in you will bring it to completion at the day of Jesus Christ.

1 Corinthians 9:24-25. Hebrews 12:1-2. 1 Timothy 6:11. Philippians 1:6.

SURELY THERE IS A FUTURE, AND YOUR HOPE
WILL NOT BE CUT OFF.

The path of the righteous is like the light of dawn, which shines brighter and brighter until full day.

From of old no one has heard or perceived by the ear, no eye has seen a God besides you, who acts for those who wait for him.

Fret not yourself because of evildoers; be not envious of wrongdoers! For they will soon fade like the grass and wither like the green herb.

Trust in the LORD, and do good; dwell in the land and befriend faithfulness. Be still before the LORD and wait patiently for him.

Proverbs 23:18. Proverbs 4:18. Isaiah 64:4. Psalm 37:1-3, 7.

KEEP YOUR LIFE FREE FROM LOVE OF MONEY,
AND BE CONTENT WITH WHAT YOU HAVE.

Judas Iscariot went to the chief priests and said, "What will you give me if I deliver [Jesus] over to you?" And they paid him thirty pieces of silver. From that moment [Judas] sought an opportunity to betray him.

He who loves money will not be satisfied with money.

Take care, and be on your guard against all covetousness, for one's life does not consist in the abundance of his possessions.

Lay up for yourselves treasures in heaven, where neither moth nor rust destroys and where thieves do not break in and steal. For where your treasure is, there your heart will be also.

But he who is noble plans noble things, and on noble things he stands.

Hebrews 13:5. Matthew 26:14-16. Ecclesiastes 5:10. Luke 12:15. Matthew 6:20-21. Isaiah 32:8.

GOD LOVES A CHEERFUL GIVER.

[Jesus] sat down opposite the treasury and watched the people putting money into the offering box. Many rich people put in large sums. And a poor widow came and put in two small copper coins, which make a penny. He called his disciples to him and said to them, "Truly, I say to you, this poor widow has put in more than all those who are contributing to the offering box. For they all contributed out of their abundance, but she out of her poverty has put in everything she had, all she had to live on."

If the readiness is there, it is acceptable according to what a person has, not according to what he does not have.

One gives freely, yet grows all the richer; another withholds what he should give, and only suffers want.

2 Corinthians 9:7. Mark 12:41-44. 2 Corinthians 8:12. Proverbs 11:24.

IF ANYONE SLAPS YOU ON THE RIGHT CHEEK, TURN TO HIM THE OTHER ALSO.

Give to the one who begs from you, and do not refuse the one who would borrow from you. You have heard that it was said, "You shall love your neighbor and hate your enemy." But I [Jesus] say to you, Love your enemies and pray for those who persecute you, so that you may be sons of your Father who is in heaven.

For he makes his sun rise on the evil and on the good, and sends rain on the just and on the unjust. If you love those who love you, what reward do you have? Do not even the tax collectors do the same? And if you greet only your brothers, what more are you doing than others?

Matthew 5:39, 42-47.

GOD SHOWS NO PARTIALITY.

If you really fulfill the royal law according to the Scripture, "You shall love your neighbor as yourself," you are doing well. But if you show partiality, you are committing sin.

For if a man wearing a gold ring and fine clothing comes into your assembly, and a poor man in shabby clothing also comes in, and if you pay attention to the one who wears the fine clothing and say, "You sit here in a good place," while you say to the poor man, "You stand over there," or, "Sit down at my feet," have you not then made distinctions among yourselves and become judges with evil thoughts? . . . You have dishonored the poor man.

Has not God chosen those who are poor in the world to be rich in faith and heirs of the kingdom, which he has promised to those who love him?

Galatians 2:6. James 2:8-9. James 2:2-4, 6. James 2:5.

KEEP AWAKE AND BE SOBER.

Put on the breastplate of faith and love, and for a helmet the hope of salvation.

Wait for the LORD; be strong, and let your heart take courage; wait for the LORD!

Once God has spoken; twice have I heard this: that power belongs to God, and that to you, O Lord, belongs steadfast love. For you will render to a man according to his work.

Oh, how abundant is your goodness, which you have stored up for those who fear you and worked for those who take refuge in you!

1 Thessalonians 5:6, 8. Psalm 27:14. Psalm 62:11-12. Psalm 31:19.

THE LORD OF HOSTS; HE IS WONDERFUL IN COUNSEL AND EXCELLENT IN WISDOM.

Does he who plows for sowing plow continually? Does he continually open and harrow his ground? When he has leveled its surface, does he not scatter dill, sow cumin, and put in wheat in rows and barley in its proper place, and emmer as the border? For he is rightly instructed; his God teaches him.

How great are your works, O LORD! Your thoughts are very deep!

Nothing is too hard for you. . . . O great and mighty God, whose name is the LORD of hosts, great in counsel and mighty in deed, whose eyes are open to all the ways of the children of man, rewarding each one according to his ways and according to the fruit of his deeds.

Isaiah 28:29, 24-26. Psalm 92:5. Jeremiah 32:17-19.

IT IS GOD WHO EXECUTES JUDGMENT, PUTTING DOWN ONE AND LIFTING UP ANOTHER.

In the hand of the LORD there is a cup with foaming wine, well mixed, and he pours out from it, and all the wicked of the earth shall drain it down to the dregs.

Truly you set them in slippery places; you make them fall to ruin. How they are destroyed in a moment, swept away utterly by terrors!

The righteous flourish like the palm tree and grow like a cedar in Lebanon.

The LORD bestows favor and honor. No good thing does he withhold from those who walk uprightly.

Psalm 75:7-8. Psalm 73:18-19. Psalm 92:12. Psalm 84:11.

BLESSED IS THE MAN WHO TRUSTS IN THE LORD, WHOSE TRUST IS THE LORD.

Daniel was . . . cast into the den of lions. . . . And a stone was brought and laid on the mouth of the den, and the king sealed it. . . . Then, at break of day, the king . . . went in haste to the den of lions. . . . He cried out in a tone of anguish, . . . "O Daniel, servant of the living God, has your God, whom you serve continually, been able to deliver you from the lions?"

Then Daniel said to the king, ". . . My God sent his angel and shut the lions' mouths, and they have not harmed me." . . . So Daniel was taken up out of the den, and no kind of harm was found on him, because he had trusted in his God.

The living God . . . delivers and rescues; he works signs and wonders in heaven and on earth, he who has saved Daniel from the power of the lions.

Jeremiah 17:7. Daniel 6:16-17, 19-23, 26-27.

WITHOUT COUNSEL PLANS FAIL, BUT WITH MANY ADVISERS THEY SUCCEED.

Remember your leaders, those who spoke to you the word of God. Consider the outcome of their way of life, and imitate their faith.

Obey your leaders and submit to them, for they are keeping watch over your souls, as those who will have to give an account. Let them do this with joy and not with groaning, for that would be of no advantage to you.

Wisdom is better than jewels, and all that you may desire cannot compare with her.

Proverbs 15:22. Hebrews 13:7, 17. Proverbs 8:11.

TEACH ME GOOD JUDGMENT AND KNOWLEDGE, FOR I BELIEVE IN YOUR COMMANDMENTS.

The law of the LORD is perfect, reviving the soul; the testimony of the LORD is sure, making wise the simple; the precepts of the LORD are right, rejoicing the heart; the commandment of the LORD is pure, enlightening the eyes; the fear of the LORD is clean, enduring forever; the rules of the LORD are true, and righteous altogether.

More to be desired are they than gold, even much fine gold; sweeter also than honey and drippings of the honeycomb. Moreover, by them is your servant warned; in keeping them there is great reward.

The word of the LORD is upright, and all his work is done in faithfulness. He loves righteousness and justice; the earth is full of the steadfast love of the LORD.

Psalm 119:66. Psalm 19:7-11. Psalm 33:4-5.

YOU SHALL HAVE NO OTHER GODS BEFORE ME.

Do what is right and good in the sight of the LORD, that it may go well with you.

The LORD your God will make you abundantly prosperous in all the work of your hand. . . . For the LORD will again take delight in prospering you . . . when you obey the voice of the LORD your God, to keep his commandments and his statutes that are written in this Book of the Law, when you turn to the LORD your God with all your heart and with all your soul.

Choose life . . . loving the LORD your God, obeying his voice and holding fast to him, for he is your life.

Exodus 20:3. Deuteronomy 6:18. Deuteronomy 30:9-10, 19-20.

[JESUS] SAID . . . "IF ANYONE WOULD COME AFTER ME, LET HIM DENY HIMSELF AND TAKE UP HIS CROSS AND FOLLOW ME."

The grace of God has appeared, bringing salvation for all people, training us to renounce ungodliness and worldly passions, and to live self-controlled, upright, and godly lives in the present age, waiting for our blessed hope, the appearing of the glory of our great God and Savior Jesus Christ, who gave himself for us to redeem us from all lawlessness and to purify for himself a people for his own possession who are zealous for good works.

Whoever is ashamed of me and of my words . . . of him will the Son of Man also be ashamed when he comes in the glory of his Father with the holy angels.

Mark 8:34. Titus 2:11-14. Mark 8:38.

GUARD THE DEPOSIT ENTRUSTED TO YOU.

Avoid the irreverent babble and contradictions of what is falsely called "knowledge."

Hezekiah . . . did what was good and right and faithful before the LORD his God. Every work that he undertook in the service of the house of God and in accordance with the law and the commandments, seeking his God, he did with all his heart, and prospered.

Put false ways far from me and graciously teach me your law! I have chosen the way of faithfulness; I set your rules before me. I cling to your testimonies, O LORD; let me not be put to shame!

1 Timothy 6:20. 2 Chronicles 31:20-21. Psalm 119:29-31.

KEEP JUSTICE, AND DO RIGHTEOUSNESS.

One who is faithful in a very little is also faithful in much, and one who is dishonest in a very little is also dishonest in much. If then you have not been faithful in the unrighteous wealth, who will entrust to you the true riches? And if you have not been faithful in that which is another's, who will give you that which is your own?

Who then is the faithful and wise manager, whom his master will set over his household, to give them their portion of food at the proper time? Blessed is that servant whom his master will find so doing when he comes. Truly, I say to you, he will set him over all his possessions.

Well done, good servant!

Isaiah 56:1. Luke 16:10-12. Luke 12:42-44. Luke 19:17.

THE WORD IS NEAR YOU, IN YOUR MOUTH
AND IN YOUR HEART
(THAT IS, THE WORD OF FAITH THAT WE PROCLAIM).

If you confess with your mouth that Jesus is Lord and believe in your heart that God raised him from the dead, you will be saved. For with the heart one believes and is justified, and with the mouth one confesses and is saved.

For the Scripture says, "Everyone who believes in him will not be put to shame." For there is no distinction between Jew and Greek; for the same Lord is Lord of all, bestowing his riches on all who call on him. For everyone who calls on the name of the Lord will be saved.

Romans 10:8-13.

YOU HAVE HEARD; NOW SEE ALL THIS; . . .

From this time forth I announce to you new things, hidden things that you have not known.

For I know the plans I have for you, declares the LORD, plans for welfare and not for evil, to give you a future and a hope.

For my thoughts are not your thoughts, neither are your ways my ways, declares the LORD. For as the heavens are higher than the earth, so are my ways higher than your ways and my thoughts than your thoughts.

Incline your ear, and come to me; hear, that your soul may live; and I will make with you an everlasting covenant.

Isaiah 48:6. Jeremiah 29:11. Isaiah 55:8-9. Isaiah 55:3.

MY SHEEP HEAR MY VOICE, AND I KNOW THEM, AND THEY FOLLOW ME.

Jesus . . . looked up and said to him, "Zacchaeus, hurry and come down, for I must stay at your house today." So he hurried and came down and received him joyfully.

Behold, I stand at the door and knock. If anyone hears my voice and opens the door, I will come in to him and eat with him, and he with me.

My people shall know my name. Therefore in that day they shall know that it is I who speak; here am I.

John 10:27. Luke 19:5-6. Revelation 3:20. Isaiah 52:6.

SOW FOR YOURSELVES RIGHTEOUSNESS;
REAP STEADFAST LOVE.

Love your enemies, and do good, and lend, expecting nothing in return, and your reward will be great, and you will be sons of the Most High, for he is kind to the ungrateful and the evil. Be merciful, even as your Father is merciful.

It is well with the man who deals generously and lends; who conducts his affairs with justice. For the righteous will never be moved; he will be remembered forever.

Give, and it will be given to you. Good measure, pressed down, shaken together, running over, will be put into your lap. With the measure you use it will be measured back to you.

Hosea 10:12. Luke 6:35-36. Psalm 112:5-6. Luke 6:38.

HONOR EVERYONE.

Be submissive to rulers and authorities, . . . be obedient, . . . be ready for every good work, . . . speak evil of no one, . . . avoid quarreling, . . . be gentle, and . . . show perfect courtesy toward all people.

[Pray] . . . for all people, for kings and all who are in high positions, that we may lead a peaceful and quiet life, godly and dignified in every way.

Give justice to the weak and the fatherless; maintain the right of the afflicted and the destitute. Rescue the weak and the needy.

Blessed is the one who considers the poor! In the day of trouble the LORD delivers him.

For God is not unjust so as to overlook your work and the love that you have shown for his name.

1 Peter 2:17. Titus 3:1-2. 1 Timothy 2:1-2. Psalm 82:3-4. Psalm 41:1. Hebrews 6:10.

BE SUBJECT TO THE GOVERNING AUTHORITIES.

For there is no authority except from God, and those that exist have been instituted by God. Therefore whoever resists the authorities resists what God has appointed, and those who resist will incur judgment.

For rulers are not a terror to good conduct, but to bad. Would you have no fear of the one who is in authority? Then do what is good, and you will receive his approval, for he is God's servant for your good. But if you do wrong, be afraid, for he does not bear the sword in vain. For he is the servant of God, an avenger who carries out God's wrath on the wrongdoer.

Be in subjection, not only to avoid God's wrath but also for the sake of conscience.

Romans 13:1-5.

PRESSING THE NOSE PRODUCES BLOOD, AND PRESSING ANGER PRODUCES STRIFE.

The beginning of strife is like letting out water, so quit before the quarrel breaks out.

Scoffers set a city aflame, but the wise turn away wrath. If a wise man has an argument with a fool, the fool only rages and laughs, and there is no quiet.

Make no friendship with a man given to anger, nor go with a wrathful man, lest you learn his ways and entangle yourself in a snare.

Let all bitterness and wrath and anger and clamor and slander be put away from you, along with all malice. Be kind to one another, tender-hearted, forgiving one another, as God in Christ forgave you.

Proverbs 30:33. Proverbs 17:14. Proverbs 29:8-9. Proverbs 22:24-25.
Ephesians 4:31-32.

DO NOT FORGET MY TEACHING—

—but let your heart keep my commandments, for length of days and years of life and peace they will add to you.

You shall therefore lay up these words of mine in your heart and in your soul, and you shall bind them as a sign on your hand, and they shall be as frontlets between your eyes.

Whatever was written in former days was written for our instruction, that through endurance and through the encouragement of the Scriptures we might have hope.

Set your minds on things that are above, not on things that are on earth. Let the word of Christ dwell in you richly, teaching and admonishing one another in all wisdom, singing psalms and hymns and spiritual songs, with thankfulness in your hearts to God.

Proverbs 3:1-2. Deuteronomy 11:18. Romans 15:4. Colossians 3:2, 16.

GREAT PEACE HAVE THOSE WHO LOVE YOUR LAW; NOTHING CAN MAKE THEM STUMBLE.

This Book of the Law shall not depart from your mouth, but you shall meditate on it day and night, so that you may be careful to do according to all that is written in it. For then you will make your way prosperous, and then you will have good success.

Have I not commanded you? Be strong and courageous. Do not be frightened, and do not be dismayed, for the LORD your God is with you wherever you go.

How can a young [person] keep his way pure? By guarding it according to your word. With my whole heart I seek you; let me not wander from your commandments! I have stored up your word in my heart, that I might not sin against you.

Psalm 119:165. Joshua 1:8-9. Psalm 119:9-11.

JUDGE NOT, AND YOU WILL NOT BE JUDGED.

Condemn not, and you will not be condemned.

With the judgment you pronounce you will be judged, and with the measure you use it will be measured to you. Why do you see the speck that is in your brother's eye, but do not notice the log that is in your own eye? Or how can you say to your brother, "Let me take the speck out of your eye," when there is the log in your own eye?

You hypocrite, first take the log out of your own eye, and then you will see clearly to take the speck out of your brother's eye.

Forgive, and you will be forgiven.

Luke 6:37. Luke 6:37. Matthew 7:2-5. Luke 6:37.

"I have stored up your word in my heart, that I might not sin against you."

AUGUST 1

CONSIDER THE WORK OF GOD: WHO CAN MAKE STRAIGHT WHAT HE HAS MADE CROOKED?

Thus says the LORD . . . "I form light and create darkness, I make well-being and create calamity, I am the LORD, who does all these things.

"Woe to him who strives with him who formed him, a pot among earthen pots! Does the clay say to him who forms it, 'What are you making?' or 'Your work has no handles'?"

For as the heavens are higher than the earth, so are my ways higher than your ways and my thoughts than your thoughts.

For those who love God all things work together for good.

O LORD, you will not restrain your mercy from me; your steadfast love and your faithfulness will ever preserve me!

Ecclesiastes 7:13. Isaiah 45:1, 7, 9. Isaiah 55:9. Romans 8:28. Psalm 40:11.

AUGUST 2

[JESUS] SAID, ". . . WHOEVER DOES THE WILL OF GOD, HE IS MY BROTHER AND SISTER AND MOTHER."

No one can lay a foundation other than that which is laid, which is Jesus Christ.

For through him we both have access in one Spirit to the Father. So then you are no longer strangers and aliens, but you are fellow citizens with the saints and members of the household of God, built on the foundation of the apostles and prophets, Christ Jesus himself being the cornerstone, in whom the whole structure, being joined together, grows into a holy temple in the Lord. In him you also are being built together into a dwelling place for God by the Spirit.

[Give] thanks to the Father, who has qualified you to share in the inheritance of the saints in light. He has delivered us from the domain of darkness and transferred us to the kingdom of his beloved Son.

Mark 3:34-35. 1 Corinthians 3:11. Ephesians 2:18-22. Colossians 1:12-13.

YOUR INIQUITIES HAVE MADE A SEPARATION BETWEEN YOU AND YOUR GOD.

Your ways and your deeds have brought this upon you. This is your doom, and it is bitter; it has reached your very heart.

All have turned aside; together they have become worthless; no one does good, not even one.

No one understands; no one seeks for God.

I know, O LORD, that the way of man is not in himself, that it is not in man who walks to direct his steps.

Correct me, O LORD, but in justice; not in your anger, lest you bring me to nothing.

Isaiah 59:2. Jeremiah 4:18. Romans 3:12. Romans 3:11. Jeremiah 10:23-24.

I WILL NOT LEAVE YOU OR FORSAKE YOU.

God is not man, that he should lie, or a son of man, that he should change his mind. Has he said, and will he not do it? Or has he spoken, and will he not fulfill it?

Know therefore that the LORD your God is God, the faithful God who keeps covenant and steadfast love with those who love him and keep his commandments.

Therefore do not be anxious about tomorrow, for tomorrow will be anxious for itself. Sufficient for the day is its own trouble.

The LORD your God is in your midst, a mighty one who will save; he will rejoice over you with gladness; he will quiet you by his love; he will exult over you with loud singing.

As for me, I would seek God, and to God would I commit my cause, who does great things and unsearchable, marvelous things without number.

Joshua 1:5. Numbers 23:19. Deuteronomy 7:9. Matthew 6:34. Zephaniah 3:17. Job 5:8-9.

WHO HAS GATHERED THE WIND IN HIS FISTS?

. . . Who has wrapped up the waters in a garment? Who has established all the ends of the earth? What is his name, and what is his son's name? Surely you know!

He who forms the mountains and creates the wind, and declares to man what is his thought, who makes the morning darkness, and treads on the heights of the earth—the LORD, the God of hosts, is his name!

The LORD is high above all nations, and his glory above the heavens! Who is like the LORD our God, who is seated on high, who looks far down on the heavens and the earth?

Proverbs 30:4. Proverbs 30:4. Amos 4:13. Psalm 113:4-6.

EVERY HOUSE IS BUILT BY SOMEONE,
BUT THE BUILDER OF ALL THINGS IS GOD.

The heavens declare the glory of God, and the sky above proclaims his handiwork.

By the word of the LORD the heavens were made, and by the breath of his mouth all their host. He gathers the waters of the sea as a heap; he puts the deeps in storehouses.

Let all the earth fear the LORD; let all the inhabitants of the world stand in awe of him! For he spoke, and it came to be; he commanded, and it stood firm.

Behold, the nations are like a drop from a bucket, and are accounted as the dust on the scales; behold, he takes up the coastlands like fine dust.

Who has measured the waters in the hollow of his hand and marked off the heavens with a span, enclosed the dust of the earth in a measure and weighed the mountains in scales and the hills in a balance?

Hebrews 3:4. Psalm 19:1. Psalm 33:6-9. Isaiah 40:15. Isaiah 40:12.

GOD IS LIGHT, AND IN HIM IS NO DARKNESS AT ALL.

If we say we have fellowship with him while we walk in darkness, we lie and do not practice the truth.

By this we know that we have come to know him, if we keep his commandments.

Whoever says "I know him" but does not keep his commandments is a liar, and the truth is not in him, but whoever keeps his word, in him truly the love of God is perfected. By this we may know that we are in him: whoever says he abides in him ought to walk in the same way in which he walked.

1 John 1:5. 1 John 1:6. 1 John 2:3-6.

WHO IS WISE AND UNDERSTANDING AMONG YOU? BY HIS GOOD CONDUCT LET HIM SHOW HIS WORKS IN THE MEEKNESS OF WISDOM.

Blessed are those whose way is blameless, who walk in the law of the LORD! Blessed are those who keep his testimonies, who seek him with their whole heart, who also do no wrong, but walk in his ways!

He leads the humble in what is right, and teaches the humble his way.

Whoever exalts himself will be humbled, and whoever humbles himself will be exalted.

The meek shall inherit the land and delight themselves in abundant peace.

James 3:13. Psalm 119:1-3. Psalm 25:9. Matthew 23:12. Psalm 37:11.

GIVE THOUGHT TO DO WHAT IS HONORABLE
IN THE SIGHT OF ALL.

You are light in the Lord. Walk as children of light (for the fruit of light is found in all that is good and right and true), and try to discern what is pleasing to the Lord.

So whatever you wish that others would do to you, do also to them.

He who walks righteously and speaks uprightly . . . will dwell on the heights; his place of defense will be the fortresses of rocks; his bread will be given him; his water will be sure.

Romans 12:17. Ephesians 5:8-10. Matthew 7:12. Isaiah 33:15-16.

OUR BLESSED HOPE, THE APPEARING OF THE GLORY
OF OUR GREAT GOD AND SAVIOR JESUS CHRIST.

In that day the deaf shall hear the words of a book, and out of their gloom and darkness the eyes of the blind shall see. The meek shall obtain fresh joy in the LORD, and the poor among mankind shall exult in the Holy One of Israel.

For the ruthless shall come to nothing and the scoffer cease, and all who watch to do evil shall be cut off. Those who go astray in spirit will come to understanding, and those who murmur will accept instruction.

Titus 2:13. Isaiah 29:18-20, 24.

DO NOT FORSAKE YOUR FRIEND AND
YOUR FATHER'S FRIEND.

Give to everyone who begs from you, and from one who takes away your goods do not demand them back. As you wish that others would do to you, do so to them.

If you love those who love you, what benefit is that to you? For even sinners love those who love them.

Bear one another's burdens, and so fulfill the law of Christ. For if anyone thinks he is something, when he is nothing, he deceives himself.

Proverbs 27:10. Luke 6:30-32. Galatians 6:2-3.

WHOEVER BRINGS BLESSING WILL BE ENRICHED,
AND ONE WHO WATERS WILL HIMSELF BE WATERED.

A man was going down from Jerusalem to Jericho, and he fell among robbers, who stripped him and beat him and departed, leaving him half dead. Now by chance a priest was going down that road, and when he saw him he passed by on the other side. So likewise a Levite . . . passed by on the other side.

But a Samaritan . . . when he saw him, he had compassion. He . . . bound up his wounds, . . . set him on his own animal and brought him to an inn and took care of him.

Which of these three, do you think, proved to be a neighbor to the man who fell among the robbers?

You go, and do likewise.

Proverbs 11:25. Luke 10:30-34, 36-37.

A STONE WILL COME BACK ON HIM
WHO STARTS IT ROLLING.

As you have done, it shall be done to you; your deeds shall return on your own head.

Beware of . . . hypocrisy. Nothing is covered up that will not be revealed, or hidden that will not be known. Therefore whatever you have said in the dark shall be heard in the light, and what you have whispered in private rooms shall be proclaimed on the housetops.

A worthless man plots evil, and his speech is like a scorching fire.

A dishonest man spreads strife, and a whisperer separates close friends.

A man of violence entices his neighbor and leads him in a way that is not good.

Keep a close watch on yourself.

Proverbs 26:27. Obadiah 15. Luke 12:1-3. Proverbs 16:27-29. 1 Timothy 4:16.

"A dishonest man spreads strife, and a whisperer separates close friends."

HE WHO REPEATS A MATTER SEPARATES CLOSE FRIENDS.

The tongue is a small member, yet it boasts of great things. How great a forest is set ablaze by such a small fire! And the tongue is a fire, a world of unrighteousness. The tongue is set among our members, staining the whole body, setting on fire the entire course of life.

Every kind of beast and bird, of reptile and sea creature, can be tamed and has been tamed by mankind, but no human being can tame the tongue. It is a restless evil, full of deadly poison.

There is one whose rash words are like sword thrusts, but the tongue of the wise brings healing. Truthful lips endure forever, but a lying tongue is but for a moment.

Proverbs 17:9. James 3:5-8. Proverbs 12:18-19.

BLESSED ARE THE PEACEMAKERS, FOR THEY SHALL BE CALLED SONS OF GOD.

You have heard that it was said, "An eye for an eye and a tooth for a tooth." But I [Jesus] say to you, "Do not resist the one who is evil. If anyone slaps you on the right cheek, turn to him the other also."

A soft answer turns away wrath, but a harsh word stirs up anger.

Whoever is slow to anger is better than the mighty, and he who rules his spirit than he who takes a city.

The wisdom from above is first pure, then peaceable, gentle, open to reason, full of mercy and good fruits, impartial and sincere. And a harvest of righteousness is sown in peace by those who make peace.

Matthew 5:9. Matthew 5:38-39. Proverbs 15:1. Proverbs 16:32. James 3:17-18.

FORGIVE, IF YOU HAVE ANYTHING AGAINST ANYONE.

If you forgive others their trespasses, your heavenly Father will also forgive you, but if you do not forgive others their trespasses, neither will your Father forgive your trespasses.

Therefore, confess your sins to one another.

For we do not have a high priest who is unable to sympathize with our weaknesses. . . . Let us then with confidence draw near to the throne of grace, that we may receive mercy and find grace to help in time of need.

Mark 11:25. Matthew 6:14-15. James 5:16. Hebrews 4:15-16.

LIVE IN HARMONY WITH ONE ANOTHER.

Do not be haughty, but associate with the lowly. Never be wise in your own sight.

Repay no one evil for evil, but give thought to do what is honorable in the sight of all. If possible, so far as it depends on you, live peaceably with all.

Let love be genuine. Abhor what is evil; hold fast to what is good. Love one another with brotherly affection. Outdo one another in showing honor. Rejoice with those who rejoice.

Behold, how good and pleasant it is when brothers dwell in unity!

Romans 12:16. Romans 12:16-18. Romans 12:9-10, 15. Psalm 133:1.

I DO NOT UNDERSTAND MY OWN ACTIONS.

For I do not do what I want, but I do the very thing I hate. For I know that nothing good dwells in me, that is, in my flesh. For I have the desire to do what is right, but not the ability to carry it out.

I do not do the good I want, but the evil I do not want is what I keep on doing. So I find it to be a law that when I want to do right, evil lies close at hand.

For it is God who works in you, both to will and to work for his good pleasure.

There is therefore now no condemnation for those who are in Christ Jesus. For the law of the Spirit of life has set you free in Christ Jesus from the law of sin and death.

Romans 7:15. Romans 7:15, 18-19, 21. Philippians 2:13. Romans 8:1-2.

BLESSED IS THE MAN WHO FEARS THE LORD,
WHO GREATLY DELIGHTS IN HIS COMMANDMENTS!

Light dawns in the darkness for the upright; he is gracious, merciful, and righteous. It is well with the man who deals generously and lends; who conducts his affairs with justice. For the righteous will never be moved; he will be remembered forever.

He is not afraid of bad news; his heart is firm, trusting in the LORD. His heart is steady; he will not be afraid, until he looks in triumph on his adversaries.

He has distributed freely; he has given to the poor; his righteousness endures forever; his horn is exalted in honor.

Psalm 112:1, 4-9.

CHOOSE THIS DAY WHOM YOU WILL SERVE.

When the rule of Rehoboam was established and he was strong, he abandoned the law of the LORD. And he did evil, for he did not set his heart to seek the LORD.

See, I am setting before you today a blessing and a curse: the blessing, if you obey the commandments of the LORD your God . . . and the curse, if you do not obey.

Therefore choose life, that you . . . may live, loving the LORD your God, obeying his voice and holding fast to him.

This is the love of God, that we keep his commandments. And his commandments are not burdensome.

Joshua 24:15. 2 Chronicles 12:1, 14. Deuteronomy 11:26-28. Deuteronomy 30:19-20.
1 John 5:3.

[BUILD] YOURSELVES UP IN YOUR MOST
HOLY FAITH.

Keep yourselves in the love of God, waiting for the mercy of our Lord Jesus Christ that leads to eternal life.

Make every effort to supplement your faith with virtue, and virtue with knowledge, and knowledge with self-control, and self-control with steadfastness, and steadfastness with godliness, and godliness with brotherly affection, and brotherly affection with love.

Now to him who is able to keep you from stumbling and to present you blameless before the presence of his glory with great joy, to the only God, our Savior, through Jesus Christ our Lord, be glory, majesty, dominion, and authority, before all time and now and forever. Amen.

Jude 20. Jude 21. 2 Peter 1:5-7. Jude 24-25.

DO NOT TURN TO MEDIUMS OR [WIZARDS]; DO NOT SEEK THEM OUT.

I am the LORD your God.

If a person turns to mediums and necromancers, whoring after them, I will set my face against that person and will cut him off from among his people.

When they say to you, "Inquire of the mediums and the necromancers who chirp and mutter," should not a people inquire of their God? Should they inquire of the dead on behalf of the living?

If we live by the Spirit, let us also walk by the Spirit.

So . . . stand firm and hold to the traditions that you were taught.

Leviticus 19:31. Leviticus 19:31. Leviticus 20:6. Isaiah 8:19. Galatians 5:25.
2 Thessalonians 2:15.

BLESSED IS THE MAN WHO WALKS NOT IN THE COUNSEL OF THE WICKED, NOR STANDS IN THE WAY OF SINNERS, NOR SITS IN THE SEAT OF SCOFFERS.

They are darkened in their understanding, alienated from the life of God because of the ignorance that is in them, due to their hardness of heart. They have become callous and have given themselves up to sensuality, greedy to practice every kind of impurity.

But that is not the way you learned Christ! . . . You . . . were taught . . . to put off your old self, which belongs to your former manner of life and is corrupt through deceitful desires, and to be renewed in the spirit of your minds, and to put on the new self, created after the likeness of God in true righteousness and holiness.

Psalm 1:1. Ephesians 4:18-24.

HEAR INSTRUCTION AND BE WISE,
AND DO NOT NEGLECT IT.

If you receive my words and treasure up my commandments with you, making your ear attentive to wisdom and inclining your heart to understanding; yes, if you call out for insight and raise your voice for understanding, if you seek it like silver and search for it as for hidden treasures, then you will understand the fear of the LORD and find the knowledge of God.

For the LORD gives wisdom; from his mouth come knowledge and understanding.

Proverbs 8:33. Proverbs 2:1-6.

MOSES WAS INSTRUCTED IN ALL THE WISDOM
OF THE EGYPTIANS, AND HE WAS MIGHTY IN HIS
WORDS AND DEEDS.

By faith Moses, when he was grown up, refused to be called the son of Pharaoh's daughter, choosing rather to be mistreated with the people of God than to enjoy the fleeting pleasures of sin. He considered the reproach of Christ greater wealth than the treasures of Egypt, for he was looking to the reward. By faith he left Egypt, not being afraid of the anger of the king, for he endured as seeing him who is invisible.

This man led [the Israelites] out, performing wonders and signs in Egypt and at the Red Sea and in the wilderness for forty years.

Now the man Moses was very meek, more than all people who were on the face of the earth.

The LORD lifts up the humble.

Acts 7:22. Hebrews 11:24-27. Acts 7:36. Numbers 12:3. Psalm 147:6.

BLESSED ARE THE MEEK, FOR THEY SHALL INHERIT THE EARTH.

Do nothing from rivalry or conceit, but in humility count others more significant than yourselves.

Do you see a man who is wise in his own eyes? There is more hope for a fool than for him.

Let no one deceive himself. If anyone among you thinks that he is wise in this age, let him become a fool that he may become wise. For the wisdom of this world is folly with God.

If anyone thinks he is something, when he is nothing, he deceives himself.

Therefore let anyone who thinks that he stands take heed lest he fall.

Matthew 5:5. Philippians 2:3. Proverbs 26:12. 1 Corinthians 3:18-19. Galatians 6:3. 1 Corinthians 10:12.

THE LORD IS MY LIGHT AND MY SALVATION; WHOM SHALL I FEAR?

The LORD is the stronghold of my life; of whom shall I be afraid?

The LORD is my rock and my fortress and my deliverer, my God, my rock, in whom I take refuge, my shield, and the horn of my salvation, my stronghold and my refuge, my savior; you save me from violence.

The LORD is my strength and my shield; in him my heart trusts, and I am helped; my heart exults, and with my song I give thanks to him.

So we can confidently say, "The Lord is my helper; I will not fear; what can man do to me?"

Psalm 27:1. Psalm 27:1. 2 Samuel 22:2-3. Psalm 28:7. Hebrews 13:6.

THE FEAR OF MAN LAYS A SNARE,
BUT WHOEVER TRUSTS IN THE LORD IS SAFE.

Joshua . . . and Caleb . . . said to all . . . the people of Israel, "The land, which we passed through to spy it out, is an exceedingly good land. If the LORD delights in us, he will bring us into this land and give it to us, a land that flows with milk and honey. Only do not rebel against the LORD. And do not fear the people of the land, for they are bread for us. Their protection is removed from them, and the LORD is with us; do not fear them."

Some trust in chariots and some in horses, but we trust in the name of the LORD our God. They collapse and fall, but we rise and stand upright.

Proverbs 29:25. Numbers 14:6-10. Psalm 20:7-8.

PRAY . . . LIKE THIS: "OUR FATHER IN HEAVEN,
HALLOWED BE YOUR NAME."

Jesus . . . lifted up his eyes to heaven, and said, "Father."

In Christ Jesus you are all sons of God, through faith.

Because you are sons, God has sent the Spirit of his Son into *your* hearts, crying, "Abba! Father!"

You have received the Spirit of adoption as sons, by whom we cry, "Abba! Father!"

"I will welcome you, and I will be a father to you, and you shall be sons and daughters to me," says the Lord Almighty.

Matthew 6:9. John 17:1. Galatians 3:26. Galatians 4:6. Romans 8:15.
2 Corinthians 6:17-18.

EVERY GOOD GIFT AND EVERY PERFECT GIFT IS FROM ABOVE, COMING DOWN FROM THE FATHER OF LIGHTS.

There are varieties of service, but the same Lord; and there are varieties of activities, but it is the same God who empowers them all in everyone.

For as in one body we have many members, and the members do not all have the same function, so we, though many, are one body in Christ, and individually members one of another. Having gifts that differ according to the grace given to us, let us use them.

The eye cannot say to the hand, "I have no need of you," nor again the head to the feet, "I have no need of you."

His divine power has granted to us all things that pertain to life and godliness, through the knowledge of him who called us to his own glory and excellence.

James 1:17. 1 Corinthians 12:5-6. Romans 12:4-6. 1 Corinthians 12:21. 2 Peter 1:3.

YOURS, O LORD, IS THE GREATNESS AND THE POWER AND THE GLORY AND THE VICTORY AND THE MAJESTY.

All that is in the heavens and in the earth is yours. Yours is the kingdom, O LORD, and you are exalted as head above all.

At the name of Jesus every knee should bow, in heaven and on earth and under the earth, and every tongue confess that Jesus Christ is Lord, to the glory of God the Father.

Your kingdom come, your will be done, on earth as it is in heaven.

For a day in your courts is better than a thousand elsewhere. I would rather be a doorkeeper in the house of my God than dwell in the tents of wickedness.

1 Chronicles 29:11. 1 Chronicles 29:11. Philippians 2:10-11. Matthew 6:10. Psalm 84:10.

SEPTEMBER 1

WE ALSO WILL SERVE THE LORD,
FOR HE IS OUR GOD.

The people said to Joshua, "The LORD our God we will serve, and his voice we will obey." So Joshua made a covenant with the people that day, and put in place statutes and rules for them.

These words that I command you today shall be on your heart. . . . Talk of them when you sit in your house, and when you walk by the way, and when you lie down, and when you rise. You shall bind them as a sign on your hand, and they shall be as frontlets between your eyes. You shall write them on the doorposts of your house and on your gates.

Do what is right and good in the sight of the LORD, that it may go well with you.

Joshua 24:18, 24-25. Deuteronomy 6:6-9, 18.

SEPTEMBER 2

THE PATH OF THE RIGHTEOUS IS LIKE THE LIGHT
OF DAWN, WHICH SHINES BRIGHTER AND BRIGHTER
UNTIL FULL DAY.

He is like a tree planted by streams of water that yields its fruit in its season, and its leaf does not wither. In all that he does, he prospers.

The wicked are not so, but are like chaff that the wind drives away. Therefore the wicked will not stand in the judgment, nor sinners in the congregation of the righteous; for the LORD knows the way of the righteous, but the way of the wicked will perish.

The LORD God is a sun and shield; the LORD bestows favor and honor. No good thing does he withhold from those who walk uprightly.

Proverbs 4:18. Psalm 1:3-6. Psalm 84:11

WHOEVER TRUSTS IN HIS OWN MIND IS A FOOL, BUT HE WHO WALKS IN WISDOM WILL BE DELIVERED.

Thus says the LORD: "Cursed is the man who trusts in man and makes flesh his strength, whose heart turns away from the LORD. He is like a shrub in the desert, and shall not see any good come. He shall dwell in the parched places of the wilderness, in an uninhabited salt land.

"Blessed is the man who trusts in the LORD, whose trust is the LORD. He is like a tree planted by water, that sends out its roots by the stream, and does not fear when heat comes, for its leaves remain green, and is not anxious in the year of drought, for it does not cease to bear fruit."

Proverbs 28:26. Jeremiah 17:5-8.

WHEN I AM AFRAID, I PUT MY TRUST IN YOU.

[Jesus] said, "Come." So Peter got out of the boat and walked on the water and came to Jesus.

But when he saw the wind, he was afraid, and beginning to sink he cried out, "Lord, save me."

Jesus immediately reached out his hand and took hold of him, saying to him, "O you of little faith, why did you doubt?"

O LORD God of hosts, who is mighty as you are, O LORD, with your faithfulness all around you? You rule the raging of the sea; when its waves rise, you still them.

Mightier than the thunders of many waters, mightier than the waves of the sea, the LORD on high is mighty!

Psalm 56:3. Matthew 14:29-31. Psalm 89:8-9. Psalm 93:4.

WHO SHALL SEPARATE US FROM THE
LOVE OF CHRIST?

Shall tribulation, or distress, or persecution, or famine, or nakedness, or danger, or sword?

I am sure that neither death nor life, nor angels nor rulers, nor things present nor things to come, nor powers, nor height nor depth, nor anything else in all creation, will be able to separate us from the love of God in Christ Jesus our Lord.

Thus says the LORD, he who created you . . . , "Fear not, for I have redeemed you; I have called you by name, you are mine. When you pass through the waters, I will be with you; and through the rivers, they shall not overwhelm you; when you walk through fire you shall not be burned, and the flame shall not consume you."

Romans 8:35. Romans 8:35, 38-39. Isaiah 43:1-2.

YOU ARE A HIDING PLACE FOR ME.

In you, O LORD, do I take refuge; let me never be put to shame; in your righteousness deliver me! Incline your ear to me; rescue me speedily! Be a rock of refuge for me, a strong fortress to save me!

You are my hiding place and my shield; I hope in your word.

Oh, how abundant is your goodness, which you have stored up for those who fear you and worked for those who take refuge in you.

This God—his way is perfect; the word of the LORD proves true; he is a shield for all those who take refuge in him.

Psalm 32:7. Psalm 31:1-2. Psalm 119:114. Psalm 31:19. Psalm 18:30.

THE LORD IS MY SHEPHERD; I SHALL NOT WANT.

He makes me lie down in green pastures. He leads me beside still waters. He restores my soul. He leads me in paths of righteousness for his name's sake.

Even though I walk through the valley of the shadow of death, I will fear no evil, for you are with me; your rod and your staff, they comfort me.

You prepare a table before me in the presence of my enemies; you anoint my head with oil; my cup overflows.

Surely goodness and mercy shall follow me all the days of my life, and I shall dwell in the house of the LORD forever.

Psalm 23:1. Psalm 23:2-6.

THE HEAVENS DECLARE THE GLORY OF GOD, AND THE SKY ABOVE PROCLAIMS HIS HANDIWORK.

For his invisible attributes, namely, his eternal power and divine nature, have been clearly perceived, ever since the creation of the world, in the things that have been made.

When I look at your heavens, the work of your fingers, the moon and the stars, which you have set in place, what is man that you are mindful of him, and the son of man that you care for him?

Those who are wise shall shine like the brightness of the sky above; and those who turn many to righteousness, like the stars forever and ever.

Psalm 19:1. Romans 1:20. Psalm 8:3-4. Daniel 12:3.

EVERY BEAST OF THE FOREST IS MINE, THE CATTLE ON A THOUSAND HILLS.

I know all the birds of the hills, and all that moves in the field is mine.

The earth is the LORD's and the fullness thereof, the world and those who dwell therein, for he has founded it upon the seas and established it upon the rivers.

In his hand are the depths of the earth; the heights of the mountains are his also. The sea is his, for he made it, and his hands formed the dry land.

Ah, Lord GOD! It is you who have made the heavens and the earth by your great power and by your outstretched arm! Nothing is too hard for you.

Psalm 50:10. Psalm 50:11. Psalm 24:1-2. Psalm 95:4-5. Jeremiah 32:17.

SEPTEMBER 10

THE RIGHTEOUS SHALL LIVE BY FAITH.

The people became impatient . . . and . . . spoke against God and against Moses, "Why have you brought us up out of Egypt to die in the wilderness? For there is no food and no water, and we loathe this worthless food."

Then the LORD sent fiery serpents among the people, and they bit the people, so that many people of Israel died.

And the people came to Moses and said, "We have sinned, for we have spoken against the LORD and against you. Pray to the LORD, that he take away the serpents from us."

So Moses prayed for the people. And the LORD said to Moses, "Make a fiery serpent and set it on a pole, and everyone who is bitten, when he sees it, shall live."

As Moses lifted up the serpent in the wilderness, so must the Son of Man be lifted up, that whoever believes in him may have eternal life.

Romans 1:17. Numbers 21:5-8. John 3:14.

MY SIN IS EVER BEFORE ME.

None is righteous, no, not one; no one understands; no one seeks for God. All have turned aside; together they have become worthless; no one does good, not even one.

All have sinned and fall short of the glory of God, and are justified by his grace as a gift, through the redemption that is in Christ Jesus.

Who is to condemn? Christ Jesus is the one who died—more than that, who was raised—who is at the right hand of God, who indeed is interceding for us.

Through this man forgiveness of sins is proclaimed to you.

Psalm 51:3. Romans 3:10-12, 23-24. Romans 8:34. Acts 13:38.

[GOD] CHOSE US IN HIM BEFORE THE FOUNDATION OF THE WORLD, THAT WE SHOULD BE HOLY AND BLAMELESS BEFORE HIM.

God gave us eternal life, and this life is in his Son.

Everyone who believes that Jesus is the Christ has been born of God.

If you confess with your mouth that Jesus is Lord and believe in your heart that God raised him from the dead, you will be saved. For with the heart one believes and is justified, and with the mouth one confesses and is saved.

I write these things to you who believe in the name of the Son of God that you may know that you have eternal life.

Ephesians 1:4. 1 John 5:11. 1 John 5:1. Romans 10:9-10. 1 John 5:13.

GOD'S LOVE HAS BEEN POURED INTO OUR HEARTS THROUGH THE HOLY SPIRIT WHO HAS BEEN GIVEN TO US.

Says the Lord GOD . . . , "I will give you a new heart, and a new spirit I will put within you. And I will remove the heart of stone from your flesh and give you a heart of flesh. And I will put my Spirit within you, and cause you to walk in my statutes and be careful to obey my rules."

I [Christ] will ask the Father, and he will give you another Helper, to be with you forever. The Helper, the Holy Spirit, whom the Father will send in my name, he will teach you all things and bring to your remembrance all that I have said to you.

The fruit of the Spirit is love, joy, peace, patience, kindness, goodness, faithfulness, gentleness, self-control; against such things there is no law.

Romans 5:5. Ezekiel 36:22, 26-27. John 14:16, 26. Galatians 5:22-23.

"And I will put my Spirit within you, and cause you to walk in my statutes and be careful to obey my rules."

DO NOT SAY, "I WILL DO TO HIM AS HE HAS DONE TO ME; I WILL PAY THE MAN BACK FOR WHAT HE HAS DONE."

Blessed are you when others revile you and persecute you and utter all kinds of evil against you falsely on my account. Rejoice and be glad, for your reward is great in heaven.

Do not let the sun go down on your anger.

Pray for those who persecute you. . . . For if you love those who love you, what reward do you have? Do not even the tax collectors do the same? And if you greet only your brothers, what more are you doing than others?

See that no one repays anyone evil for evil, but always seek to do good to one another and to everyone.

Proverbs 24:29. Matthew 5:11-12. Ephesians 4:26. Matthew 5:44, 46-47.
1 Thessalonians 5:15.

A FRIEND LOVES AT ALL TIMES.

Jonathan, Saul's son, delighted much in David.

Jonathan loved him as his own soul.

Two are better than one, because they have a good reward for their toil. For if they fall, one will lift up his fellow. But woe to him who is alone when he falls and has not another to lift him up! Again, if two lie together, they keep warm, but how can one keep warm alone?

Jonathan said to David, "Whatever you say, I will do for you."

Greater love has no one than this, that someone lay down his life for his friends.

Proverbs 17:17. 1 Samuel 19:1. 1 Samuel 18:1. Ecclesiastes 4:9-11. 1 Samuel 20:4.
John 15:13.

[LOVE] DOES NOT REJOICE AT WRONGDOING, BUT REJOICES WITH THE TRUTH.

To show partiality is not good, but for a piece of bread a man will do wrong.

Justice is turned back, and righteousness stands far away; for truth has stumbled in the public squares, and uprightness cannot enter.

Learn to do good; seek justice, correct oppression; bring justice to the fatherless, plead the widow's cause.

Love kindness, and . . . walk humbly with your God.

1 Corinthians 13:6. Proverbs 28:21. Isaiah 59:14. Isaiah 1:17. Micah 6:8.

WHOEVER BELIEVES IN THE SON HAS ETERNAL LIFE; WHOEVER DOES NOT OBEY THE SON SHALL NOT SEE LIFE, BUT THE WRATH OF GOD REMAINS ON HIM.

Note then the kindness and the severity of God: severity toward those who have fallen, but God's kindness to you, provided you continue in his kindness.

His anger is but for a moment, and his favor is for a lifetime.

The Lord is . . . patient toward you, not wishing that any should perish, but that all should reach repentance.

Draw near to God, and he will draw near to you.

He is gracious and merciful, slow to anger, and abounding in steadfast love.

John 3:36. Romans 11:22. Psalm 30:5. 2 Peter 3:9. James 4:8. Joel 2:13.

THE EARTH SHALL BE FULL OF THE KNOWLEDGE OF THE LORD.

In that day the deaf shall hear the words of a book, and out of their gloom and darkness the eyes of the blind shall see. The meek shall obtain fresh joy in the LORD, and the poor among mankind shall exult in the Holy One of Israel.

The wolf shall dwell with the lamb, and the leopard shall lie down with the young goat, and the calf and the lion and the fattened calf together; and a little child shall lead them.

The cow and the bear shall graze; their young shall lie down together; and the lion shall eat straw like the ox. The nursing child shall play over the hole of the cobra, and the weaned child shall put his hand on the adder's den. They shall not hurt or destroy.

Isaiah 11:9. Isaiah 29:18-19. Isaiah 11:6-9.

FOREVER, O LORD, YOUR WORD IS FIRMLY FIXED IN THE HEAVENS.

All flesh is like grass and all its glory like the flower of grass. The grass withers, and the flower falls, but the word of the Lord remains forever.

The word of God is living and active, sharper than any two-edged sword, piercing to the division of soul and of spirit, of joints and of marrow, and discerning the thoughts and intentions of the heart.

All Scripture is breathed out by God and profitable for teaching, for reproof, for correction, and for training in righteousness, that the man of God may be competent, equipped for every good work.

Psalm 119:89. 1 Peter 1:24-25. Hebrews 4:12. 2 Timothy 3:16.

ONE LORD, ONE FAITH, ONE BAPTISM.

One Lord. Jesus said . . . , "I am the way, and the truth, and the life. No one comes to the Father except through me. I am the good shepherd. . . . There will be one flock, one shepherd."

One faith. Faith is the assurance of things hoped for, the conviction of things not seen. Therefore do not throw away your confidence, which has a great reward.

One baptism. Baptized . . . in order that . . . we too might walk in newness of life.

Ephesians 4:5. Ephesians 4:5. John 14:6. John 10:11, 16. Ephesians 4:5. Hebrews 11:1. Hebrews 10:35. Ephesians 4:5. Romans 6:3-4.

TO THE PURE, ALL THINGS ARE PURE.

Whatever is true, whatever is honorable, whatever is just, whatever is pure, whatever is lovely, whatever is commendable, if there is any excellence, if there is anything worthy of praise, think about these things.

But to the defiled and unbelieving, nothing is pure; but both their minds and their consciences are defiled. They profess to know God, but they deny him by their works. They are detestable, disobedient, unfit for any good work.

The words of his mouth are trouble and deceit; he has ceased to act wisely and do good. He plots trouble while on his bed; he sets himself in a way that is not good; he does not reject evil.

Those who live according to the flesh set their minds on the things of the flesh, but those who live according to the Spirit set their minds on the things of the Spirit.

Titus 1:15. Philippians 4:8. Titus 1:15-16. Psalm 36:3-4. Romans 8:5.

I CAN DO ALL THINGS THROUGH [CHRIST] WHO STRENGTHENS ME.

For this very reason, make every effort to supplement your faith with virtue, and virtue with knowledge, and knowledge with self-control, and self-control with steadfastness, and steadfastness with godliness, and godliness with brotherly affection, and brotherly affection with love.

For if these qualities are yours and are increasing, they keep you from being ineffective or unfruitful in the knowledge of our Lord Jesus Christ. For whoever lacks these qualities is so nearsighted that he is blind, having forgotten that he was cleansed from his former sins.

Be all the more diligent to make your calling and election sure, for if you practice these qualities you will never fall. For in this way, there will be richly provided for you an entrance into the eternal kingdom of our Lord and Savior Jesus Christ.

Philippians 4:13. 2 Peter 1:5-11.

REMEMBER . . . YOUR CREATOR IN THE DAYS OF YOUR YOUTH.

Give to him glorious praise!

Say to God, "How awesome are your deeds! So great is your power that your enemies come cringing to you. All the earth worships you and sings praises to you; they sing praises to your name."

O LORD, you have searched me and known me! You know when I sit down and when I rise up; you discern my thoughts from afar. You search out my path and my lying down and are acquainted with all my ways. Such knowledge is too wonderful for me; it is high; I cannot attain it.

I give thanks to you, O Lord my God, with my whole heart, and I will glorify your name forever.

Ecclesiastes 12:1. Psalm 66:2-4. Psalm 139:1-3, 6. Psalm 86:12.

IT IS THE TIME TO SEEK THE LORD.

Sow for yourselves righteousness; reap steadfast love; break up your fallow ground . . . that he may come and rain righteousness upon you.

There is salvation in no one else, for there is no other name under heaven given among men by which we must be saved.

The righteousness of God has been manifested apart from the law . . . through faith in Jesus Christ for all who believe. There is no distinction: for all have sinned and fall short of the glory of God, and are justified by his grace as a gift.

May the God of endurance and encouragement grant you to live in such harmony with one another, in accord with Christ Jesus, that together you may with one voice glorify the God and Father of our Lord Jesus Christ.

Hosea 10:12. Hosea 10:12. Acts 4:12. Romans 3:21-24. Romans 15:5-6.

ONE'S PRIDE WILL BRING HIM LOW, BUT HE WHO IS LOWLY IN SPIRIT WILL OBTAIN HONOR.

The disciples came to Jesus, saying, "Who is the greatest in the kingdom of heaven?" And calling to him a child, [Jesus] put him in the midst of them and said, ". . . Whoever humbles himself like this child is the greatest in the kingdom of heaven."

Talk no more so very proudly, let not arrogance come from your mouth; for the LORD is a God of knowledge, and by him actions are weighed. Pride goes before destruction, and a haughty spirit before a fall. It is better to be of a lowly spirit with the poor than to divide the spoil with the proud.

Whoever heeds instruction is on the path to life.

The LORD lifts up the humble.

For though the LORD is high, he regards the lowly.

Proverbs 29:23. Matthew 18:1-4. 1 Samuel 2:3. Proverbs 16:18-19. Proverbs 10:17. Psalm 147:6. Psalm 138:6.

CHILDREN, OBEY YOUR PARENTS IN EVERYTHING, FOR THIS PLEASES THE LORD.

Honor your father and mother (this is the first commandment with a promise), that it may go well with you and that you may live long in the land.

Listen to your father who gave you life, and do not despise your mother when she is old.

By wisdom a house is built, and by understanding it is established; by knowledge the rooms are filled with all precious and pleasant riches.

A wise man is full of strength, and a man of knowledge enhances his might, for by wise guidance you can wage your war, and in abundance of counselors there is victory.

Colossians 3:20. Ephesians 6:2-3. Proverbs 23:22. Proverbs 24:3-6.

I WILL BLESS THE LORD AT ALL TIMES; HIS PRAISE SHALL CONTINUALLY BE IN MY MOUTH.

My soul makes its boast in the LORD; let the humble hear and be glad. Oh, magnify the LORD with me, and let us exalt his name together!

I sought the LORD, and he answered me and delivered me from all my fears. Those who look to him are radiant, and their faces shall never be ashamed.

My soul waits for the LORD; he is *my* help and *my* shield.

My heart is glad in him, because *I* trust in his holy name.

Let your steadfast love, O LORD, be upon *me*, even as *I* hope in you.

Psalm 34:1. Psalm 34:2-5. Psalm 33:20-22.

GIVE, AND IT WILL BE GIVEN TO YOU.

Rebekah . . . came out with her water jar on her shoulder. . . . She went down to the spring and filled her jar and came up. Then the servant ran to meet her and said, "Please give me a little water to drink from your jar."

She said, "Drink, my lord." . . . When she had finished giving him a drink, she said, "I will draw water for your camels also, until they have finished drinking." So she quickly emptied her jar into the trough and ran again to the well to draw water, and she drew for all his camels.

. . . When the camels had finished drinking, the man took [out] a gold ring weighing a half shekel, and two bracelets for her arms weighing ten gold shekels.

Whatever you do, work heartily, as for the Lord and not for men.

Give, and it will be given to you.

Luke 6:38. Genesis 24:15-20, 22. Colossians 3:23. Luke 6:38.

REFRAIN FROM ANGER, AND FORSAKE WRATH!

Scoffers set a city aflame, but the wise turn away wrath.

Whoever is slow to anger has great understanding, but he who has a hasty temper exalts folly.

So flee youthful passions and pursue righteousness, faith, love, and peace, along with those who call on the Lord from a pure heart. Have nothing to do with foolish, ignorant controversies; you know that they breed quarrels.

Be careful to devote yourself to good works. These things are excellent and profitable for people.

Psalm 37:8. Proverbs 29:8. Proverbs 14:29. 2 Timothy 2:22, 23. Titus 3:8.

WRATH IS CRUEL, ANGER IS OVERWHELMING, BUT WHO CAN STAND BEFORE JEALOUSY?

Let us not become conceited, provoking one another, envying one another.

A tranquil heart gives life to the flesh, but envy makes the bones rot.

If you have bitter jealousy and selfish ambition in your hearts, do not boast and be false to the truth. This is not the wisdom that comes down from above, but is earthly, unspiritual, demonic. For where jealousy and selfish ambition exist, there will be disorder and every vile practice.

But the wisdom from above is first pure, then peaceable, gentle, open to reason, full of mercy and good fruits, impartial and sincere.

And a harvest of righteousness is sown in peace by those who make peace.

Proverbs 27:4. Galatians 5:26. Proverbs 14:30. James 3:14-18.

"Whatever you do, work heartily, as for the Lord and not for men."

OCTOBER 1

PUT ON . . . COMPASSIONATE HEARTS, KINDNESS.

King [David] said, "Is there not still someone of the house of Saul, that I may show the kindness of God to him?"

If anyone has the world's goods and sees his brother in need, yet closes his heart against him, how does God's love abide in him?

For you know the grace of our Lord Jesus Christ, that though he was rich, yet for your sake he became poor, so that you by his poverty might become rich.

Do not neglect to do good and to share what you have, for such sacrifices are pleasing to God.

Give to the one who begs from you, and do not refuse the one who would borrow from you.

Blessed are the merciful.

Colossians 3:12. 2 Samuel 9:3. 1 John 3:17. 2 Corinthians 8:9. Hebrews 13:16. Matthew 5:42. Matthew 5:7.

OCTOBER 2

TRUST IN THE LORD, AND DO GOOD.

Do all things without grumbling or questioning.

The tongue of the righteous is choice silver; the heart of the wicked is of little worth.

Bless those who persecute you; bless and do not curse them.

Doing wrong is like a joke to a fool, but wisdom is pleasure to a man of understanding.

Do not say, "I will do to him as he has done to me; I will pay the man back for what he has done."

Be still before the LORD and wait patiently for him; fret not yourself over the one who prospers in his way, over the man who carries out evil devices!

Psalm 37:3. Philippians 2:14. Proverbs 10:20. Romans 12:14. Proverbs 10:23. Proverbs 24:29. Psalm 37:7.

TO DO RIGHTEOUSNESS AND JUSTICE IS MORE ACCEPTABLE TO THE LORD THAN SACRIFICE.

The LORD works righteousness and justice for all who are oppressed. He made known his ways to Moses, his acts to the people of Israel. The LORD is merciful and gracious, slow to anger and abounding in steadfast love.

Gracious is the LORD, and righteous; our God is merciful.

Your steadfast love is great above the heavens; your faithfulness reaches to the clouds.

I will ponder the way that is blameless. . . . I will walk with integrity of heart within my house; I will not set before my eyes anything that is worthless.

The earth, O LORD, is full of your steadfast love; teach me your statutes! I incline my heart to perform your statutes forever, to the end.

Proverbs 21:3. Psalm 103:6-8. Psalm 116:5. Psalm 108:4. Psalm 101:2-3. Psalm 119:64, 112.

AT ONE TIME YOU WERE DARKNESS, BUT NOW YOU ARE LIGHT IN THE LORD.

Walk as children of light (for the fruit of light is found in all that is good and right and true), and try to discern what is pleasing to the Lord.

While there is jealousy and strife among you, are you not of the flesh and behaving only in a human way?

Take no part in the unfruitful works of darkness.

Do not be conformed to this world, but be transformed by the renewal of your mind, that by testing you may discern what is the will of God, what is good and acceptable and perfect.

Live self-controlled, upright, and godly lives.

Ephesians 5:8. Ephesians 5:8-10. 1 Corinthians 3:3. Ephesians 5:11. Romans 12:2. Titus 2:12.

DO NOT LIE TO ONE ANOTHER . . .

You have put off the old self with its practices and have put on the new self, which is being renewed in knowledge after the image of its creator.

If anyone does not stumble in what he says, he is a perfect man, able also to bridle his whole body. If we put bits into the mouths of horses so that they obey us, we guide their whole bodies as well. Look at the ships also: though they are so large and are driven by strong winds, they are guided by a very small rudder wherever the will of the pilot directs.

So also the tongue is a small member, yet it boasts of great things. How great a forest is set ablaze by such a small fire! And the tongue is a fire, a world of unrighteousness. The tongue is set among our members, staining the whole body, setting on fire the entire course of life.

Let your "yes" be yes and your "no" be no, so that you may not fall under condemnation.

Colossians 3:9. Colossians 3:9-10. James 3:2-6. James 5:12.

WE ALL STUMBLE IN MANY WAYS.

But the LORD upholds the righteous. The steps of a man are established by the LORD, when he delights in his way; though he fall, he shall not be cast headlong, for the LORD upholds his hand. The LORD loves justice; he will not forsake his saints.

[God] will not let your foot be moved; he who keeps you will not slumber.

Let us walk properly as in the daytime . . . not in quarreling and jealousy.

My eyes are toward you, O GOD, my Lord.

Your word is a lamp to my feet and a light to my path.

James 3:2. Psalm 37:17, 23-24, 28. Psalm 121:3. Romans 13:13. Psalm 141:8. Psalm 119:105.

IN THE DAY OF MY TROUBLE I CALL UPON YOU, FOR YOU ANSWER ME.

The LORD will fulfill his purpose for me; your steadfast love, O LORD, endures forever. Do not forsake the work of your hands.

How precious to me are your thoughts, O God!

Incline your ear, O LORD, and answer me, for I am poor and needy. Preserve my life, for I am godly; save your servant, who trusts in you—you are my God.

Be gracious to me, O Lord, for to you do I cry all the day. Gladden the soul of your servant, for to you, O Lord, do I lift up my soul. For you, O Lord, are good and forgiving, abounding in steadfast love to all who call upon you.

Give ear, O LORD, to my prayer; listen to my plea for grace.

Psalm 86:7. Psalm 138:8. Psalm 139:17. Psalm 86:1-6.

THE LORD KNOWS HOW TO RESCUE THE GODLY FROM TRIALS.

Blessed is the man who remains steadfast under trial, for when he has stood the test he will receive the crown of life, which God has promised to those who love him.

Let no one say when he is tempted, "I am being tempted by God," for God cannot be tempted with evil, and he himself tempts no one. But each person is tempted when he is lured and enticed by his own desire. Then desire when it has conceived gives birth to sin, and sin when it is fully grown brings forth death.

Do not be deceived. . . . Every good gift and every perfect gift is from above, coming down from the Father of lights with whom there is no variation or shadow due to change.

2 Peter 2:9. James 1:12-17.

THERE WILL BE FALSE TEACHERS
AMONG YOU...

[They] will secretly bring in destructive heresies, even denying the Master who bought them, bringing upon themselves swift destruction. And many will follow their sensuality, and because of them the way of truth will be blasphemed. And in their greed they will exploit you with false words. Their condemnation from long ago is not idle, and their destruction is not asleep.

Many deceivers have gone out into the world, those who do not confess the coming of Jesus Christ in the flesh. Such a one is the deceiver and the antichrist. Watch yourselves.

Disaster pursues sinners, but the righteous are rewarded with good.

2 Peter 2:1. 2 Peter 2:1-3. 2 John 7-8. Proverbs 13:21.

YOU MUST BE BORN AGAIN.

Truly, truly, I [Jesus] say to you, whoever believes has eternal life.

My Father, who has given them to me, is greater than all, and no one is able to snatch them out of the Father's hand.

Whoever believes in him is not condemned, but whoever does not believe is condemned already, because he has not believed in the name of the only Son of God.

And this is the judgment: the light has come into the world, and people loved the darkness rather than the light because their works were evil. For everyone who does wicked things hates the light and does not come to the light, lest his works should be exposed.

But whoever does what is true comes to the light, so that it may be clearly seen that his works have been carried out in God.

John 3:7. John 6:47. John 10:29. John 3:18-21.

LET YOUR LIGHT SHINE BEFORE OTHERS, SO THAT THEY MAY SEE YOUR GOOD WORKS AND GIVE GLORY TO YOUR FATHER WHO IS IN HEAVEN.

Jesus spoke to [the Pharisees], saying, "I am the light of the world. Whoever follows me will not walk in darkness, but will have the light of life."

You are all children of light, children of the day.

At one time you were darkness, but now you are light in the Lord. Walk as children of light . . . that you may be blameless and innocent, children of God without blemish in the midst of a crooked and twisted generation, among whom you shine as lights in the world.

No one after lighting a lamp puts it in a cellar or under a basket, but on a stand, so that those who enter may see the light. If then your whole body is full of light, having no part dark, it will be wholly bright, as when a lamp with its rays gives you light.

God is light, and in him is no darkness at all.

Matthew 5:16. John 8:12. 1 Thessalonians 5:5. Ephesians 5:8. Philippians 2:15. Luke 11:33, 36. 1 John 1:5.

YOUR HANDS HAVE MADE AND FASHIONED ME.

Put false ways far from me and graciously teach me your law! I have chosen the way of faithfulness; I set your rules before me.

Forever, O LORD, your word is firmly fixed in the heavens. Your faithfulness endures to all generations; you have established the earth, and it stands fast. By your appointment they stand this day, for all things are your servants.

I will never forget your precepts, for by them you have given me life.

Uphold me according to your promise, that I may live, and let me not be put to shame in my hope!

Psalm 119:73. Psalm 119:29-30, 89-91, 93, 116.

OCTOBER 13

DO NOT GRUMBLE AGAINST ONE ANOTHER . . . SO THAT YOU MAY NOT BE JUDGED.

Judge not, that you be not judged. For with the judgment you pronounce you will be judged, and with the measure you use it will be measured to you. So then let us pursue what makes for peace and for mutual upbuilding. Do nothing from rivalry or conceit, but in humility count others more significant than yourselves. Let each of you look not only to his own interests, but also to the interests of others. Have this mind among yourselves, which is yours in Christ Jesus, who, though he was in the form of God, did not count equality with God a thing to be grasped, but made himself nothing, taking the form of a servant.

Who are you to judge your neighbor?

James 5:9. Matthew 7:1-2. Romans 14:19. Philippians 2:3-7. James 4:12.

OCTOBER 14

AT THE NAME OF JESUS EVERY KNEE SHOULD BOW, IN HEAVEN AND ON EARTH AND UNDER THE EARTH, AND EVERY TONGUE CONFESS THAT JESUS CHRIST IS LORD, TO THE GLORY OF GOD THE FATHER.

He must reign until he has put all his enemies under his feet. The last enemy to be destroyed is death. Christ . . . far above all rule and authority and power and dominion, and above every name that is named, not only in this age but also in the one to come.

Our Lord Jesus Christ . . . he who is the blessed and only Sovereign, the King of kings and Lord of lords, who alone has immortality, who dwells in unapproachable light, whom no one has ever seen or can see. To him be honor and eternal dominion. Amen.

According to his promise we are waiting for new heavens and a new earth in which righteousness dwells.

Philippians 2:10-11. 1 Corinthians 15:25-26. Ephesians 1:20-21. 1 Timothy 6:14-16. 2 Peter 3:13.

BARTIMAEUS, A BLIND BEGGAR . . . WAS SITTING BY THE ROADSIDE.

When he heard that it was Jesus of Nazareth, he began to cry out and say, "Jesus, Son of David, have mercy on me!"

Jesus stopped and said, "Call him." And they called the blind man, saying to him, "Take heart. Get up; he is calling you." And throwing off his cloak, he sprang up and came to Jesus.

And Jesus said to him, "What do you want me to do for you?"

The blind man said to him, "Rabbi, let me recover my sight."

Jesus said to him, "Go your way; your faith has made you well." And immediately he recovered his sight and followed him on the way.

When [Jesus] saw the crowds, he had compassion for them, because they were harassed and helpless, like sheep without a shepherd.

Mark 10:46. Mark 10:47, 49-52. Matthew 9:36.

GOD HAS SPOKEN IN HIS HOLINESS.

Who is like you, O LORD, among the gods? Who is like you, majestic in holiness, awesome in glorious deeds, doing wonders?

There is none holy like the LORD; there is none besides you; there is no rock like our God.

The word of the LORD is upright, and all his work is done in faithfulness. He loves righteousness and justice.

This God—his way is perfect; the word of the LORD proves true; he is a shield for all those who take refuge in him.

The LORD of hosts is exalted in justice, and the Holy God shows himself holy in righteousness.

Exalt the LORD our God; worship at his footstool! Holy is he!

Psalm 60:6. Exodus 15:11. 1 Samuel 2:2. Psalm 33:4-5. Psalm 18:30. Isaiah 5:16. Psalm 99:5.

OCTOBER 17

THERE IS GREAT GAIN IN GODLINESS
WITH CONTENTMENT.

Job . . . said: "Oh, that I were as in the months of old, as in the days when God watched over me, when his lamp shone upon my head, and by his light I walked through darkness, as I was in my prime, when the friendship of God was upon my tent, when the Almighty was yet with me, when my children were all around me."

The LORD restored the fortunes of Job, when he had prayed for his friends. And the LORD gave Job twice as much as he had before. The LORD blessed the latter days of Job more than his beginning.

Be patient. . . . See how the farmer waits for the precious fruit of the earth, being patient about it, until it receives the early and the late rains. You also, be patient. . . . Do not grumble against one another. . . . As an example of suffering and patience . . . take the prophets who spoke in the name of the Lord. Behold, we consider those blessed who remained steadfast. You have heard of the steadfastness of Job, and you have seen the purpose of the Lord, how the Lord is compassionate and merciful.

1 Timothy 6:6. Job 29:1-5. Job 42:10, 12. James 5:7-11.

OCTOBER 18

THE LORD PRESERVES ALL WHO LOVE HIM.

All your works shall give thanks to you, O LORD, and all your saints shall bless you! They shall speak of the glory of your kingdom and tell of your power, to make known to the children of man your mighty deeds, and the glorious splendor of your kingdom. Your kingdom is an everlasting kingdom, and your dominion endures throughout all generations.

The eyes of all look to you, and you give them their food in due season. You open your hand; you satisfy the desire of every living thing.

The LORD is righteous in all his ways and kind in all his works. The LORD is near to all who call on him, to all who call on him in truth.

Psalm 145:20. Psalm 145:10-13, 15-18.

THE LORD YOUR GOD IS IN YOUR MIDST, A GREAT AND AWESOME GOD.

The Rock, his work is perfect, for all his ways are justice. A God of faithfulness and without iniquity, just and upright is he.

With God are wisdom and might; he has counsel and understanding. God chose what is foolish in the world to shame the wise; God chose what is weak in the world to shame the strong; God chose what is low and despised in the world, even things that are not, to bring to nothing things that are, so that no human being might boast in the presence of God.

Oh, the depth of the riches and wisdom and knowledge of God! How unsearchable are his judgments and how inscrutable his ways!

For as the heavens are higher than the earth, so are *his* ways higher than *our* ways and *his* thoughts than *our* thoughts.

All the paths of the LORD are steadfast love and faithfulness, for those who keep his covenant and his testimonies.

Deuteronomy 7:21. Deuteronomy 32:3-4. Job 12:13. 1 Corinthians 1:27-29.
Romans 11:33. Isaiah 55:9. Psalm 25:10.

ASCRIBE GREATNESS TO OUR GOD!

There is none like God . . . who rides through the heavens to your help, through the skies in his majesty. The eternal God is your dwelling place, and underneath are the everlasting arms.

For the eyes of the LORD run to and fro throughout the whole earth, to give strong support to those whose heart is blameless toward him.

Yours, O LORD, is the greatness and the power and the glory and the victory and the majesty, for all that is in the heavens and in the earth is yours. Yours is the kingdom, O LORD, and you are exalted as head above all. Both riches and honor come from you, and you rule over all. In your hand are power and might, and in your hand it is to make great and to give strength to all.

Deuteronomy 32:3. Deuteronomy 33:26-27. 2 Chronicles 16:9. 1 Chronicles 29:11-12.

EAT HONEY, FOR IT IS GOOD, AND THE DRIPPINGS OF THE HONEYCOMB ARE SWEET TO YOUR TASTE.

Know that wisdom is such to your soul; if you find it, there will be a future, and your hope will not be cut off. Yes, if you call out for insight and raise your voice for understanding, if you seek it like silver and search for it as for hidden treasures, then you will understand the fear of the LORD and find the knowledge of God.

For the LORD gives wisdom; from his mouth come knowledge and understanding; he stores up sound wisdom for the upright; he is a shield to those who walk in integrity, guarding the paths of justice and watching over the way of his saints. Then you will understand righteousness and justice and equity, every good path; for wisdom will come into your heart, and knowledge will be pleasant to your soul; discretion will watch over you, understanding will guard you, delivering you from the way of evil, from men of perverted speech.

Proverbs 24:13. Proverbs 24:14. Proverbs 2:3-12.

OCTOBER 22

CONTRIBUTE TO THE NEEDS OF THE SAINTS AND SEEK TO SHOW HOSPITALITY.

[Abraham] lifted up his eyes and looked, and behold, three men were standing in front of him. When he saw them, he ran from the tent door to meet them . . . and said, "O Lord, if I have found favor in your sight, do not pass by your servant. Let a little water be brought, and wash your feet, and rest yourselves under the tree, while I bring a morsel of bread, that you may refresh yourselves, and after that you may pass on. . . ."

So they said, "Do as you have said." And Abraham went quickly into the tent to Sarah and said, "Quick! Three seahs of fine flour! Knead it, and make cakes."

Do not neglect to show hospitality to strangers, for thereby some have entertained angels unawares.

Romans 12:13. Genesis 18:2-6. Hebrews 13:2.

WHETHER YOU EAT OR DRINK, OR WHATEVER YOU DO, DO ALL TO THE GLORY OF GOD.

Be watchful, stand firm in the faith . . . be strong. Let all that you do be done in love.

Look carefully then how you walk, not as unwise but as wise, making the best use of the time, because the days are evil. Therefore do not be foolish, but understand what the will of the Lord is.

Abound more and more, with knowledge and all discernment, so that you may approve what is excellent, and so be pure and blameless for the day of Christ, filled with the fruit of righteousness that comes through Jesus Christ, to the glory and praise of God.

1 Corinthians 10:31. 1 Corinthians 16:13-14. Ephesians 5:15-17. Philippians 1:9-11.

NO TEMPTATION HAS OVERTAKEN YOU THAT IS NOT COMMON TO MAN.

Jesus was led up by the Spirit into the wilderness to be tempted by the devil.

The devil took him to a very high mountain and showed him all the kingdoms of the world and their glory. And he said to him, "All these I will give you, if you will fall down and worship me."

Then Jesus said to him, "Be gone, Satan! For it is written, 'You shall worship the Lord your God and him only shall you serve.'"

God is faithful, and he will not let you be tempted beyond your ability, but with the temptation he will also provide the way of escape, that you may be able to endure it.

Because [Jesus] himself has suffered when tempted, he is able to help those who are being tempted.

1 Corinthians 10:13. Matthew 4:1, 8-10. 1 Corinthians 10:13. Hebrews 2:18.

OUR GOD IS IN THE HEAVENS;
HE DOES ALL THAT HE PLEASES.

When God saw what [the people of Nineveh] did, how they turned from their evil way, God relented of the disaster that he had said he would do to them, and he did not do it. But it displeased Jonah exceedingly, and he was angry.

Woe to him who strives with him who formed him, a pot among earthen pots! Does the clay say to him who forms it, "What are you making?" or "Your work has no handles?"

Who are you, O man, to answer back to God? Will what is molded say to its molder, "Why have you made me like this?" Has the potter no right over the clay?

O LORD, you are our Father; we are the clay, and you are our potter; we are all the work of your hand.

Psalm 115:3. Jonah 3:10. Jonah 4:1. Isaiah 45:9. Romans 9:20-21. Isaiah 64:8.

WHEN WORDS ARE MANY,
TRANSGRESSION IS NOT LACKING.

Let every person be quick to hear, slow to speak, slow to anger.

Whoever is slow to anger is better than the mighty, and he who rules his spirit than he who takes a city.

Whoever restrains his lips is prudent.

Whoever guards his mouth preserves his life; he who opens wide his lips comes to ruin.

Set a guard, O LORD, over my mouth; keep watch over the door of my lips!

Proverbs 10:19. James 1:19. Proverbs 16:32. Proverbs 10:19. Proverbs 13:3.
Psalm 141:3.

I KNOW YOUR SITTING DOWN AND YOUR GOING OUT AND COMING IN.

You discern my thoughts from afar. You search out my path and my lying down and are acquainted with all my ways. Even before a word is on my tongue, behold, O LORD, you know it altogether.

Where shall I go from your Spirit? Or where shall I flee from your presence? If I ascend to heaven, you are there! If I make my bed in Sheol, you are there! If I take the wings of the morning and dwell in the uttermost parts of the sea, even there your hand shall lead me, and your right hand shall hold me.

2 Kings 19:27. Psalm 139:2-4, 7-10.

TRULY, YOUR GOD IS GOD OF GODS AND LORD OF KINGS.

Blessed be the name of God forever and ever, to whom belong wisdom and might. He changes times and seasons; he removes kings and sets up kings; he gives wisdom to the wise and knowledge to those who have understanding.

He reveals deep and hidden things; he knows what is in the darkness, and the light dwells with him.

All the inhabitants of the earth are accounted as nothing, and he does according to his will among the host of heaven and among the inhabitants of the earth.

Daniel 2:47. Daniel 2:20-22. Daniel 4:35.

I AM GOD ALMIGHTY; WALK BEFORE ME, AND BE BLAMELESS.

Grow in the grace and knowledge of our Lord and Savior Jesus Christ.

Do not let your adorning be external—the braiding of hair and the putting on of gold jewelry, or the clothing you wear—but let your adorning be the hidden person of the heart with the imperishable beauty of a gentle and quiet spirit, which in God's sight is very precious.

The wisdom from above is first pure, then peaceable, gentle, open to reason, full of mercy and good fruits, impartial and sincere. And a harvest of righteousness is sown in peace by those who make peace.

The LORD takes pleasure in his people; he adorns the humble with salvation.

Genesis 17:1. 2 Peter 3:18. 1 Peter 3:3-4. James 3:17-18. Psalm 149:4.

WHEN YOU PRAY—

—you must not be like the hypocrites. For they love to stand and pray in the synagogues and at the street corners, that they may be seen by others. Truly, I say to you, they have received their reward.

But when you pray, go into your room and shut the door and pray to your Father who is in secret. And your Father who sees in secret will reward you.

The LORD is good to those who wait for him, to the soul who seeks him. It is good that one should wait quietly for the salvation of the LORD.

Matthew 6:5. Matthew 6:5-6. Lamentations 3:25-26.

GOD IS A RIGHTEOUS JUDGE, AND A GOD WHO FEELS INDIGNATION EVERY DAY.

Say among the nations, "The LORD reigns! Yes, the world is established; it shall never be moved; he will judge the peoples with equity."

The LORD makes poor and makes rich; he brings low and he exalts. He raises up the poor from the dust; he lifts the needy from the ash heap to make them sit with princes and inherit a seat of honor. For the pillars of the earth are the LORD's, and on them he has set the world.

He will guard the feet of his faithful ones, but the wicked shall be cut off in darkness, for not by might shall a man prevail.

You, O LORD, reign forever; your throne endures to all generations.

Psalm 7:11. Psalm 96:10. 1 Samuel 2:7-9. Lamentations 5:19.

> "He lifts the needy from the ash heap to make them sit with princes and inherit a seat of honor."

IF WE SAY WE HAVE NO SIN, WE DECEIVE OURSELVES, AND THE TRUTH IS NOT IN US.

All have sinned and fall short of the glory of God. From within, out of the heart of man, come evil thoughts . . . coveting, wickedness, deceit, sensuality, envy, slander, pride, foolishness.

The wicked are like the tossing sea; for it cannot be quiet, and its waters toss up mire and dirt. They hated knowledge and did not choose the fear of the LORD, would have none of my counsel and despised all my reproof, therefore they shall eat the fruit of their way, and have their fill of their own devices. The iniquities of the wicked ensnare.

If we confess our sins, he is faithful and just to forgive us our sins and to cleanse us from all unrighteousness.

I am writing these things to you so that you may not sin. But if anyone does sin, we have an advocate with the Father, Jesus Christ the righteous.

1 John 1:8. Romans 3:23. Mark 7:21-22. Isaiah 57:20. Proverbs 1:29-31. Proverbs 5:22. 1 John 1:9. 1 John 2:1.

THE LORD WAITS TO BE GRACIOUS TO YOU, AND THEREFORE HE EXALTS HIMSELF TO SHOW MERCY TO YOU.

The LORD is a God of justice; blessed are all those who wait for him.

Come now, let us reason together, says the LORD: though your sins are like scarlet, they shall be as white as snow; though they are red like crimson, they shall become like wool.

Now in Christ Jesus you who once were far off have been brought near by the blood of Christ.

Isaiah 30:18. Isaiah 30:18. Isaiah 1:18. Ephesians 2:13.

DO NOT BE ANXIOUS ABOUT TOMORROW.

It is the LORD who goes before you. He will be with you; he will not leave you or forsake you. Do not fear or be dismayed.

The LORD your God is in your midst . . . he will rejoice over you with gladness; he will quiet you by his love; he will exult over you with loud singing.

Trust in the LORD with all your heart, and do not lean on your own understanding. In all your ways acknowledge him, and he will make straight your paths.

Commit your way to the LORD; trust in him, and he will act.

The steadfast love of the LORD never ceases; his mercies never come to an end; they are new every morning; great is his faithfulness.

Matthew 6:34. Deuteronomy 31:8. Zephaniah 3:17. Proverbs 3:5-6. Psalm 37:5. Lamentations 3:22-23.

THE LORD IS GOOD, A STRONGHOLD IN THE DAY OF TROUBLE; HE KNOWS THOSE WHO TAKE REFUGE IN HIM.

O God, we have heard with our ears, our fathers have told us, what deeds you performed in their days, in the days of old: you with your own hand drove out the nations, but them you planted; you afflicted the peoples, but them you set free; for not by their own sword did they win the land, nor did their own arm save them, but your right hand and your arm, and the light of your face, for you delighted in them.

The LORD . . . their stronghold in the time of trouble.

For you, O LORD, do I wait; it is you, O Lord my God, who will answer.

Nahum 1:7. Psalm 44:1-3. Psalm 37:39. Psalm 38:15.

THE LORD IS THE TRUE GOD; HE IS THE LIVING GOD AND THE EVERLASTING KING.

It is he who made the earth by his power, who established the world by his wisdom, and by his understanding stretched out the heavens. When he utters his voice, there is a tumult of waters in the heavens, and he makes the mist rise from the ends of the earth. He makes lightning for the rain, and he brings forth the wind from his storehouses.

The LORD is high above all nations, and his glory above the heavens! Our God is in the heavens; he does all that he pleases.

The LORD is our judge; the LORD is our lawgiver; the LORD is our king; he will save us.

There is none like you, O LORD; you are great, and your name is great in might.

Jeremiah 10:10. Jeremiah 10:12-13. Psalm 113:4. Psalm 115:3. Isaiah 33:22. Jeremiah 10:6.

MAY THE LORD OF PEACE HIMSELF GIVE YOU PEACE AT ALL TIMES IN EVERY WAY.

Some went down to the sea in ships, doing business on the great waters; they saw the deeds of the LORD, his wondrous works in the deep. For he commanded and raised the stormy wind, which lifted up the waves of the sea. They mounted up to heaven; they went down to the depths; their courage melted away in their evil plight; they reeled and staggered like drunken men and were at their wits' end.

Then they cried to the LORD in their trouble, and he delivered them from their distress. He made the storm be still, and the waves of the sea were hushed. Then they were glad that the waters were quiet, and he brought them to their desired haven.

The living God . . . delivers and rescues; he works signs and wonders in heaven and on earth.

2 Thessalonians 3:16. Psalm 107:23-30. Daniel 6:26-27.

THE LORD DELIGHTS IN YOU.

Can a woman forget her nursing child . . . ? Even these may forget, yet I will not forget you. Behold, I have engraved you on the palms of my hands.

I will betroth you to me forever. I will betroth you to me in righteousness and in justice, in steadfast love and in mercy. I will betroth you to me in faithfulness. And you shall know the LORD.

You shall be mine, says the LORD of hosts, in the day when I make up my treasured possession.

You are precious in my eyes, and honored, and I love you.

Isaiah 62:4. Isaiah 49:15-16. Hosea 2:19-20. Malachi 3:17. Isaiah 43:4.

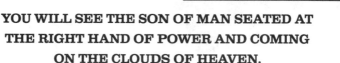

YOU WILL SEE THE SON OF MAN SEATED AT THE RIGHT HAND OF POWER AND COMING ON THE CLOUDS OF HEAVEN.

As the lightning comes from the east and shines as far as the west, so will be the coming of the Son of Man. . . . *You* will see the Son of Man coming on the clouds of heaven with power and great glory.

Therefore, stay awake, for you do not know on what day your Lord is coming. But know this, that if the master of the house had known in what part of the night the thief was coming, he would have stayed awake and would not have let his house be broken into. Therefore you also must be ready, for the Son of Man is coming at an hour you do not expect.

Blessed are those servants whom the master finds awake when he comes.

Matthew 26:64. Matthew 24:27, 30, 42-44. Luke 12:37.

I PRESS ON TOWARD THE GOAL.

Forgetting what lies behind and straining forward to what lies ahead.

Every athlete exercises self-control in all things. They do it to receive a perishable wreath, but we an imperishable.

Let us also lay aside every weight, and sin which clings so closely, and let us run with endurance the race that is set before us, looking to Jesus, the founder and perfecter of our faith.

Let your manner of life be worthy of the gospel of Christ.

Henceforth there is laid up for *you* the crown of righteousness, which the Lord, the righteous judge, will award to *you* on that Day, and not only to *you* but also to all who have loved his appearing.

Philippians 3:14. Philippians 3:13. 1 Corinthians 9:25. Hebrews 12:1-2.
Philippians 1:27. 2 Timothy 4:8.

"Let us run with endurance the race that is set before us, looking to Jesus, the founder and perfecter of our faith."

PRAISE AND EXTOL AND HONOR THE KING OF HEAVEN, FOR ALL HIS WORKS ARE RIGHT AND HIS WAYS ARE JUST.

The God who made the world and everything in it, being Lord of heaven and earth, does not live in temples made by man, nor is he served by human hands, as though he needed anything, since he himself gives to all mankind life and breath and everything.

And he made from one man every nation of mankind to live on all the face of the earth, having determined allotted periods and the boundaries of their dwelling place, that they should seek God, in the hope that they might feel their way toward him and find him. Yet he is actually not far from each one of us, for "in him we live and move and have our being."

Who is the man who fears the LORD? Him will he instruct in the way that he should choose.

Daniel 4:37. Acts 17:24-28. Psalm 25:12.

IT IS NOT AN ENEMY WHO TAUNTS ME . . . IT IS . . . MY COMPANION, MY FAMILIAR FRIEND.

A messenger came to David, saying, "The hearts of the men of Israel have gone after Absalom."

I [Jeremiah] hear many whispering. Terror is on every side! "Denounce him! Let us denounce him!" say all my close friends, watching for my fall. "Perhaps he will be deceived; then we can overcome him and take our revenge on him."

Love the LORD, all you his saints! The LORD preserves the faithful but abundantly repays the one who acts in pride. Be strong, and let your heart take courage, all you who wait for the LORD!

God is *your* helper; the Lord is the upholder of *your* life.

The LORD is with *you*.

Psalm 55:12-13. 2 Samuel 15:13. Jeremiah 20:10. Psalm 31:23-24. Psalm 54:4. Jeremiah 20:11.

NOVEMBER 12

LOVE YOUR ENEMIES, DO GOOD TO THOSE WHO HATE YOU.

Bless those who curse you, pray for those who abuse you.

To one who strikes you on the cheek, offer the other also, and from one who takes away your cloak do not withhold your tunic either. Give to everyone who begs from you, and from one who takes away your goods do not demand them back.

As you wish that others would do to you, do so to them.

Luke 6:27. Luke 6:28-31.

NOVEMBER 13

STRIVE FOR PEACE WITH EVERYONE.

The LORD is gracious and merciful, slow to anger and abounding in steadfast love.

Be imitators of God, as beloved children. And walk in love, as Christ loved us and gave himself up for us, a fragrant offering and sacrifice to God.

Be kind to one another, tenderhearted, forgiving one another, as God in Christ forgave you.

Having purified your souls by your obedience to the truth for a sincere brotherly love, love one another earnestly from a pure heart,

Hebrews 12:14. Psalm 145:8. Ephesians 5:1-2. Ephesians 4:32. 1 Peter 1:22.

AS THE FATHER HAS LOVED ME,
SO HAVE I LOVED YOU. ABIDE IN MY LOVE.

If you keep my commandments, you will abide in my love, just as I have kept my Father's commandments and abide in his love. These things I have spoken to you, that my joy may be in you, and that your joy may be full.

This is my commandment, that you love one another as I have loved you. Greater love has no one than this, that someone lay down his life for his friends.

Faith, hope, and love abide, these three; but the greatest of these is love.

John 15:9. John 15:10-13. 1 Corinthians 13:13.

A GOOD NAME IS BETTER THAN
PRECIOUS OINTMENT.

Trust in the LORD, and do good. You will find favor and good success in the sight of God and man.

You will understand righteousness and justice and equity, every good path.

Light dawns in the darkness for the upright; he is gracious, merciful, and righteous.

The path of the upright is a level highway.

The integrity of the upright guides them, but the crookedness of the treacherous destroys them.

The upright gives thought to his ways.

How forceful are upright words!

[The LORD] stores up sound wisdom for the upright; he is a shield to those who walk in integrity.

Psalm 37:3. Proverbs 3:4. Proverbs 2:9. Psalm 112:4. Proverbs 15:19. Proverbs 11:3. Proverbs 21:29. Job 6:25. Proverbs 2:7.

MY HEART IS STEADFAST, O GOD! I WILL SING AND MAKE MELODY WITH ALL MY BEING!

Awake, O harp and lyre! I will awake the dawn!

I will give thanks to you, O LORD, among the peoples; I will sing praises to you among the nations. For your steadfast love is great above the heavens; your faithfulness reaches to the clouds.

Send out your light and your truth; let them lead me; let them bring me to your holy hill and to your dwelling! Then I will go to the altar of God, to God my exceeding joy, and I will praise you with the lyre, O God, my God.

Psalm 108:1. Psalm 108:2-4. Psalm 43:3-4.

HAVE FAITH IN GOD.

Abraham believed God, and it was counted to him as righteousness. . . . We say that faith was counted to Abraham as righteousness. How then was it counted to him?

In hope he believed against hope, that he should become the father of many nations, as he had been told.

No distrust made him waver concerning the promise of God, but he grew strong in his faith as he gave glory to God, fully convinced that God was able to do what he had promised. That is why his faith was "counted to him as righteousness."

But the words "it was counted to him" were not written for his sake alone, but for ours also. It will be counted to us who believe in him who raised from the dead Jesus our Lord, who was delivered up for our trespasses and raised for our justification.

Therefore, since we have been justified by faith, we have peace with God through our Lord Jesus Christ.

Mark 11:22. Romans 4:3, 9-10, 18, 20-25. Romans 5:1.

HE GAVE HIS ONLY SON.

His invisible attributes, namely, his eternal power and divine nature, have been clearly perceived, ever since the creation of the world, in the things that have been made.

Day to day pours out speech, and night to night reveals knowledge.

When I look at your heavens, the work of your fingers, the moon and the stars, which you have set in place, what is man that you are mindful of him?

Just as sin came into the world through one man [Adam], and death through sin, and so death spread to all men because all sinned.

God so loved the world, that he gave his only Son, that whoever believes in him should not perish but have eternal life.

John 3:16. Romans 1:20. Psalm 19:2. Psalm 8:3, 4. Romans 5:12. John 3:16.

WITHOUT FAITH IT IS IMPOSSIBLE TO
PLEASE [GOD].

Whoever would draw near to God must believe that he exists and that he rewards those who seek him.

[Build] yourselves up in your most holy faith.

In all circumstances take up the shield of faith, with which you can extinguish all the flaming darts of the evil one.

As it is written, "The righteous shall live by faith."

By it the people of old received their commendation. Abel . . . Noah . . . Abraham . . . Moses. . . . These all died in faith. . . . Therefore God is not ashamed to be called their God.

Everyone who acknowledges me before men, I also will acknowledge before my Father who is in heaven, but whoever denies me before men, I also will deny before my Father who is in heaven.

Hebrews 11:6. Hebrews 11:6. Jude 20. Ephesians 6:16. Romans 1:17.
Hebrews 11:2, 4, 7-8, 23, 13, 16. Matthew 10:32-33.

WHAT GOD IS THERE IN HEAVEN OR ON EARTH
WHO CAN DO SUCH WORKS AND
MIGHTY ACTS AS YOURS?

Let the heavens praise your wonders, O LORD, your faithfulness in the assembly of the holy ones! For who in the skies can be compared to the LORD? Who among the heavenly beings is like the LORD, a God greatly to be feared in the council of the holy ones, and awesome above all who are around him?

O LORD God of hosts, who is mighty as you are, O LORD, with your faithfulness all around you?

Deuteronomy 3:24. Psalm 89:5-8.

GOD CREATED MAN IN HIS OWN IMAGE.

Thus says the LORD, who created the heavens (he is God!), who formed the earth and made it (he established it; he did not create it empty, he formed it to be inhabited!): "I am the LORD, and there is no other."

The LORD looks down from heaven; he sees all the children of man; from where he sits enthroned he looks out on all the inhabitants of the earth, he who fashions the hearts of them all and observes all their deeds.

Know that the LORD, he is God! It is he who made us, and we are his; we are his people, and the sheep of his pasture.

Oh come, let us worship and bow down; let us kneel before the LORD, our Maker!

Genesis 1:27. Isaiah 45:18. Psalm 33:13-15. Psalm 100:3. Psalm 95:6.

YOU ARE THE LIGHT OF THE WORLD.

Do all things without grumbling or questioning, that you may be blameless and innocent, children of God without blemish in the midst of a crooked and twisted generation, among whom you shine as lights in the world, holding fast to the word of life.

Those who are wise shall shine like the brightness of the sky above; and those who turn many to righteousness, like the stars forever and ever.

The LORD bestows favor and honor. No good thing does he withhold from those who walk uprightly.

Matthew 5:14. Philippians 2:14-16. Daniel 12:3. Psalm 84:11.

LET ANOTHER PRAISE YOU, AND
NOT YOUR OWN MOUTH.

Woe to those who are wise in their own eyes, and shrewd in their own sight!

If anyone imagines that he knows something, he does not yet know as he ought to know.

There is more hope for a fool than for him.

What do you have that you did not receive? If then you received it, why do you boast as if you did not receive it?

Everyone who exalts himself will be humbled, but the one who humbles himself will be exalted.

Submit yourselves therefore to God. . . . Draw near to God, and he will draw near to you.

Proverbs 27:2. Isaiah 5:21. 1 Corinthians 8:2. Proverbs 26:12. 1 Corinthians 4:7. Luke 18:14. James 4:7-8.

THE WORDS OF THE WISE ARE LIKE GOADS.

Wisdom is better than jewels, and all that you may desire cannot compare with her. I, wisdom, dwell with prudence, and I find knowledge and discretion.

The fear of the LORD is the beginning of wisdom, and the knowledge of the Holy One is insight. For by me your days will be multiplied, and years will be added to your life.

Blessed is the one who listens to me, watching daily at my gates, waiting beside my doors. For whoever finds me finds life and obtains favor from the LORD.

Ecclesiastes 12:11. Proverbs 8:11-12. Proverbs 9:10-11. Proverbs 8:34-35.

HE WHO FOLLOWS WORTHLESS PURSUITS
LACKS SENSE.

Trust in the LORD with all your heart, and do not lean on your own understanding. In all your ways acknowledge him, and he will make straight your paths. Be not wise in your own eyes; fear the LORD, and turn away from evil.

Is not [the LORD] your father, who created you, who made you and established you? Remember the days of old; consider the years of many generations; ask your father, and he will show you, your elders, and they will tell you.

Listen to advice and accept instruction that you may gain wisdom in the future.

The way of a fool is right in his own eyes, but a wise man listens to advice.

Proverbs 12:11. Proverbs 3:5-7. Deuteronomy 32:6-7. Proverbs 19:20.
Proverbs 12:15.

COMMIT YOUR WORK TO THE LORD, AND YOUR PLANS WILL BE ESTABLISHED.

Whatever your hand finds to do, do it with your might.

Whatever you do, work heartily, as for the Lord and not for men, knowing that from the Lord you will receive the inheritance as your reward. You are serving the Lord Christ.

Respect those who labor among you and are over you in the Lord and admonish you . . . esteem them very highly in love because of their work. Be at peace among yourselves.

Apply your heart to instruction and your ear to words of knowledge.

In due season *you* will reap if *you* do not give up.

Proverbs 16:3. Ecclesiastes 9:10. Colossians 3:23-24. 1 Thessalonians 5:12-13.
Proverbs 23:12. Galatians 6:9.

GRACIOUS WORDS ARE PURE.

Rejoice. Aim for restoration, comfort one another, agree with one another, live in peace; and the God of love and peace will be with you.

In the house of the righteous there is much treasure.

Behold, how good and pleasant it is when brothers dwell in unity! It is like the dew of Hermon, which falls on the mountains of Zion!

To make an apt answer is a joy to a man, and a word in season, how good it is!

Better is a little with the fear of the LORD than great treasure and trouble with it. Better is a dinner of herbs where love is than a fattened ox and hatred with it.

A gentle tongue is a tree of life, but perverseness in it breaks the spirit.

Proverbs 15:26. 2 Corinthians 13:11. Proverbs 15:6. Psalm 133:1, 3. Proverbs 15:23.
Proverbs 15:16-17. Proverbs 15:4.

DELIGHT YOURSELF IN THE LORD, AND HE WILL GIVE YOU THE DESIRES OF YOUR HEART.

Commit your way to the LORD; trust in him, and he will act. Wait for the LORD and keep his way, and he will exalt you to inherit the land; you will look on when the wicked are cut off.

I have seen a wicked, ruthless man, spreading himself like a green laurel tree. But he passed away, and behold, he was no more; though I sought him, he could not be found.

Mark the blameless and behold the upright, for there is a future for the man of peace.

Psalm 37:4. Psalm 37:5, 34-37.

DO NOT BE HAUGHTY, BUT ASSOCIATE WITH THE LOWLY.

Has not God chosen those who are poor in the world to be rich in faith and heirs of the kingdom, which he has promised to those who love him?

Blessed is the one who considers the poor!

Whoever has two tunics is to share with him who has none, and whoever has food is to do likewise.

Do not neglect to do good and to share what you have, for such sacrifices are pleasing to God.

Whoever gives to the poor will not want.

Whoever has a bountiful eye will be blessed, for he shares his bread with the poor.

Romans 12:16. James 2:5. Psalm 41:1. Luke 3:11. Hebrews 13:16. Proverbs 28:27. Proverbs 22:9.

BE CONTENT WITH WHAT YOU HAVE.

Someone in the crowd said to [Jesus], "Teacher, tell my brother to divide the inheritance with me."

[Jesus] said to him, "Man, who made me a judge or arbitrator over you? . . . Take care, and be on your guard against all covetousness, for one's life does not consist in the abundance of his possessions."

Keep your life free from love of money.

There is great gain in godliness with contentment, for we brought nothing into the world, and we cannot take anything out of the world. But if we have food and clothing, with these we will be content.

Hebrews 13:5. Luke 12:13-15. Hebrews 13:5. 1 Timothy 6:6-8.

> "One's life does not consist in the abundance of his possessions."

DECEMBER 1

EVERY ONE OF YOU SHALL REVERE HIS MOTHER AND HIS FATHER.

You shall stand up before the gray head and honor the face of an old man.

Do not rebuke an older man but encourage him as you would a father, younger men as brothers, older women as mothers, younger women as sisters in all purity.

Let no one despise you for your youth, but set the believers an example in speech, in conduct, in love, in faith, in purity. Keep a close watch on yourself.

Leviticus 19:3, 32. 1 Timothy 5:1-2. 1 Timothy 4:12, 16.

DECEMBER 2

BLESSED BE THE LORD, WHO DAILY BEARS US UP; GOD IS OUR SALVATION.

Jesus said . . . "All that the Father gives me will come to me, and whoever comes to me I will never cast out. For I have come down from heaven, not to do my own will but the will of him who sent me. . . . This is the will of my Father, that everyone who looks on the Son and believes in him should have eternal life."

"I am the good shepherd. I know my own and my own know me. . . . I lay down my life for the sheep."

Trust in the LORD with all your heart, and do not lean on your own understanding. In all your ways acknowledge him, and he will make straight your paths.

Psalm 68:19. John 6:35, 37-38, 40. John 10:14-15. Proverbs 3:5-6.

WITH US IS THE LORD OUR GOD, TO HELP US AND TO FIGHT OUR BATTLES.

Blessed is he whose help is the God of Jacob, whose hope is in the LORD his God.

Behold, the eye of the LORD is on those who fear him, on those who hope in his steadfast love, that he may deliver their soul from death and keep them alive in famine.

[God] has said, "I will never leave you nor forsake you." So we can confidently say, "The Lord is my helper; I will not fear; what can man do to me?"

2 Chronicles 32:8. Psalm 146:5. Psalm 33:18-19. Hebrews 13:5-6.

THE LORD IS GOOD.

God heard the voice of the boy, and the angel of God called to Hagar from heaven and said to her, "What troubles you, Hagar? Fear not, for God has heard the voice of the boy where he is." Then God opened her eyes, and she saw a well of water. And she went and filled the skin with water and gave the boy a drink.

The LORD is good to all, and his mercy is over all that he has made. All your works shall give thanks to you, O LORD, and all your saints shall bless you!

Nahum 1:7. Genesis 21:17, 19. Psalm 145:9-10.

A GOOD MAN WILL BE FILLED WITH THE FRUIT OF HIS WAYS.

[God] will render to each one according to his works: to those who by patience in well-doing seek for glory and honor and immortality, he will give eternal life; but for those who are self-seeking and do not obey the truth, but obey unrighteousness, there will be wrath and fury. There will be tribulation and distress for every human being who does evil . . . but glory and honor and peace for everyone who does good.

Everyone who acknowledges [Jesus] before men, [Jesus] also will acknowledge before *his* Father who is in heaven.

The LORD knows the way of the righteous.

Proverbs 14:14. Romans 2:6-10. Matthew 10:32. Psalm 1:6.

UNDERNEATH ARE THE EVERLASTING ARMS.

When [Peter] saw the wind, he was afraid, and beginning to sink he cried out, "Lord, save me." Jesus immediately reached out his hand and took hold of him, saying to him, "O you of little faith, why did you doubt?"

The steps of a man are established by the LORD, when he delights in his way; though he fall, he shall not be cast headlong, for the LORD upholds his hand.

Humble yourselves, therefore, under the mighty hand of God . . . casting all your anxieties on him, because he cares for you.

Deuteronomy 33:27. Matthew 14:30-31. Psalm 37:23-24. 1 Peter 5:6-7.

WALK BEFORE GOD IN THE LIGHT OF LIFE.

I have taught you the way of wisdom; I have led you in the paths of uprightness. When you walk, your step will not be hampered, and if you run, you will not stumble. Keep hold of instruction; do not let go; guard her, for she is your life.

Bless our God, O peoples; let the sound of his praise be heard, who has kept our soul among the living and has not let our feet slip.

Psalm 56:13. Proverbs 4:11-13. Psalm 66:8-9.

GREAT IS THE LORD, AND GREATLY
TO BE PRAISED.

The LORD made the heavens. Splendor and majesty are before him; strength and joy are in his place.

Ascribe to the LORD, O clans of the peoples, ascribe to the LORD glory and strength! Ascribe to the LORD the glory due his name; bring an offering and come before him! Worship the LORD in the splendor of holiness.

Let the heavens be glad, and let the earth rejoice, and let them say among the nations, "The LORD reigns!"

1 Chronicles 16:25. 1 Chronicles 16:26-29, 31.

GREAT IS OUR LORD, AND ABUNDANT IN POWER.

Bless the LORD, O my soul! O LORD my God, you are very great! You are clothed with splendor and majesty. I will sing to the LORD as long as I live; I will sing praise to my God while I have being.

O LORD, God of our fathers, are you not God in heaven? You rule over all the kingdoms of the nations. In your hand are power and might, so that none is able to withstand you.

O Lord GOD, you have only begun to show your servant your greatness and your mighty hand.

I will ponder all your work, and meditate on your mighty deeds. You are the God who works wonders.

Psalm 147:5. Psalm 104:1, 33. 2 Chronicles 20:6. Deuteronomy 3:24.
Psalm 77:12, 14.

DECEMBER 10

BLESSED BE THE NAME OF GOD FOREVER AND EVER, TO WHOM BELONG WISDOM AND MIGHT.

The heavens are yours; the earth also is yours; the world and all that is in it, you have founded them. The north and the south, you have created them; Tabor and Hermon joyously praise your name.

You have a mighty arm; strong is your hand, high your right hand. Righteousness and justice are the foundation of your throne; steadfast love and faithfulness go before you. Blessed are the people who know the festal shout, who walk, O LORD, in the light of your face, who exult in your name all the day and in your righteousness are exalted. You are the glory of their strength; by your favor our horn is exalted.

[You] give wisdom to the wise and knowledge to those who have understanding.

Daniel 2:20. Psalm 89:11-17. Daniel 2:21.

[GOD] IS ABLE TO DO FAR MORE ABUNDANTLY THAN ALL THAT WE ASK OR THINK.

The earth is the LORD's and the fullness thereof, the world and those who dwell therein.

He made the moon to mark the seasons; the sun knows its time for setting. *He made* darkness, and it is night, when all the beasts of the forest creep about. The young lions roar for their prey, seeking their food from God. When the sun rises, they steal away and lie down in their dens.

These all look to *God*, to give them their food in due season. When *he gives* it to them, they gather it up; when *he opens his* hand, they are filled with good things.

Therefore do not be anxious about tomorrow. But seek first the kingdom of God and his righteousness.

Ephesians 3:20. Psalm 24:1. Psalm 104:19-22, 27-28. Matthew 6:34, 33.

WE HAVE COME TO KNOW AND TO BELIEVE THE LOVE THAT GOD HAS FOR US.

In this the love of God was made manifest among us, that God sent his only Son into the world, so that we might live through him. In this is love, not that we have loved God but that he loved us and sent his Son to be the propitiation for our sins.

He chose us in him before the foundation of the world, that we should be holy and blameless before him. In love he predestined us for adoption through Jesus Christ, according to the purpose of his will.

As a father shows compassion to his children, so the LORD shows compassion to those who fear him.

1 John 4:16. 1 John 4:9-10. Ephesians 1:4-5. Psalm 103:13.

YOUR NAME, O LORD, ENDURES FOREVER, YOUR RENOWN, O LORD, THROUGHOUT ALL AGES.

Lord, you have been our dwelling place in all generations. Before the mountains were brought forth, or ever you had formed the earth and the world, from everlasting to everlasting you are God. A thousand years in your sight are but as yesterday when it is past, or as a watch in the night.

Of old you laid the foundation of the earth, and the heavens are the work of your hands. They will perish, but you will remain; they will all wear out like a garment. You will change them like a robe, and they will pass away, but you are the same, and your years have no end.

Psalm 135:13. Psalm 90:1-2, 4. Psalm 102:25-27.

PRAISE THE LORD! PRAISE GOD IN HIS SANCTUARY; PRAISE HIM IN HIS MIGHTY HEAVENS!

Praise him for his mighty deeds; praise him according to his excellent greatness!

Praise him with trumpet sound; praise him with lute and harp! Praise him with tambourine and dance; praise him with strings and pipe! Praise him with sounding cymbals; praise him with loud clashing cymbals!

Let everything that has breath praise the LORD! Praise the LORD!

Psalm 150:1. Psalm 150:2-6.

IN EVERYTHING BY PRAYER AND SUPPLICATION
WITH THANKSGIVING LET YOUR REQUESTS
BE MADE KNOWN TO GOD.

Seek the LORD and his strength; seek his presence continually!

When you pray, go into your room and shut the door and pray to your Father who is in secret. And your Father who sees in secret will reward you.

Draw near to God, and he will draw near to you.

Do not be anxious about anything. . . . And the peace of God, which surpasses all understanding, will guard your hearts and your minds in Christ Jesus.

The prayer of a righteous person has great power.

Philippians 4:6. 1 Chronicles 16:11. Matthew 6:6. James 4:8. Philippians 4:6-7. James 5:16.

THE WORD BECAME FLESH AND
DWELT AMONG US.

[Jesus] shall stand and shepherd his flock in the strength of the LORD, in the majesty of the name of the LORD his God.

Jesus . . . had come from God and was going back to God.

He must reign until he has put all his enemies under his feet. The last enemy to be destroyed is death. When all things are subjected to him, then the Son himself will also be subjected to [God] who put all things in subjection under him, that God may be all in all.

Be exalted, O God, above the heavens! Let your glory be over all the earth!

John 1:14. Micah 5:4. John 13:3. 1 Corinthians 15:25-26, 28. Psalm 108:5.

YOU SHALL CALL HIS NAME JESUS, FOR HE WILL SAVE HIS PEOPLE FROM THEIR SINS.

He was wounded for our transgressions; he was crushed for our iniquities; upon him was the chastisement that brought us peace, and with his stripes we are healed. All we like sheep have gone astray; we have turned—every one—to his own way; and the LORD has laid on him the iniquity of us all.

He was oppressed, and he was afflicted, yet he opened not his mouth; like a lamb that is led to the slaughter, and like a sheep that before its shearers is silent, so he opened not his mouth. By oppression and judgment he was taken away . . . stricken for [our] transgressions. . . .

He has appeared once for all . . . to put away sin by the sacrifice of himself. Through this man forgiveness of sins is proclaimed to you.

Matthew 1:21. Isaiah 53:5-8. Hebrews 9:26. Acts 13:38.

WONDERFUL COUNSELOR.

. . . Christ, in whom are hidden all the treasures of wisdom and knowledge. The Spirit of the LORD shall rest upon him, the Spirit of wisdom and understanding, the Spirit of counsel and might, the Spirit of knowledge and the fear of the LORD.

His divine power has granted to us all things that pertain to life and godliness, through the knowledge of him who called us to his own glory and excellence, by which he has granted to us his precious and very great promises, so that through them you may become partakers of the divine nature.

Isaiah 9:6. Colossians 2:2-3. Isaiah 11:2. 2 Peter 1:3-4.

**WHEN CHRIST CAME INTO THE WORLD, HE SAID, . . .
"BEHOLD, I HAVE COME TO DO YOUR WILL, O GOD."**

The Spirit of the Lord GOD is upon me, because the LORD has anointed me

> to bring good news to the poor; he has sent me to bind up the brokenhearted,
>
> to proclaim liberty to the captives, and the opening of the prison to those who are bound;
>
> to proclaim the year of the LORD's favor, and the day of vengeance of our God;
>
> to comfort all who mourn; to grant to those who mourn in Zion—
>> to give them a beautiful headdress instead of ashes,
>> the oil of gladness instead of mourning,
>> the garment of praise instead of a faint spirit;

> that they may be called oaks of righteousness, the planting of the LORD, that he may be glorified.

Hebrews 10:5, 7. Isaiah 61:1-3.

MIGHTY GOD.

. . . Christ . . . far above all rule and authority and power and dominion, and above every name that is named, not only in this age but also in the one to come. And [God] put all things under his feet.

Gird your sword on your thigh, O mighty one, in your splendor and majesty! In your majesty ride out victoriously for the cause of truth and meekness and righteousness. . . . Your throne, O God, is forever and ever. The scepter of your kingdom is a scepter of uprightness.

He is the radiance of the glory of God and the exact imprint of his nature, and he upholds the universe by the word of his power.

Isaiah 9:6. Ephesians 1:20-22. Psalm 45:3-4, 6. Hebrews 1:3.

GOD DID NOT SEND HIS SON INTO THE WORLD TO CONDEMN THE WORLD, BUT IN ORDER THAT THE WORLD MIGHT BE SAVED THROUGH HIM.

To us a child is born, to us a son is given; and the government shall be upon his shoulder, and his name shall be called

Wonderful Counselor

Mighty God

Everlasting Father

Prince of Peace.

You are in Christ Jesus, who became to us wisdom from God, righteousness and sanctification and redemption.

No one can lay a foundation other than that which is laid, which is Jesus Christ.

Of the increase of his government and of peace there will be no end.

John 3:17. Isaiah 9:6. 1 Corinthians 1:30. 1 Corinthians 3:11. Isaiah 9:7.

DECEMBER 22

EVERLASTING FATHER.

[God] has spoken to us by his Son, whom he appointed the heir of all things, through whom also he created the world.

He is before all things, and in him all things hold together. In him the whole fullness of deity dwells bodily.

Of the Son [God] says, . . . "You, Lord, laid the foundation of the earth in the beginning, and the heavens are the work of your hands; they will perish, but you remain; they will all wear out like a garment, like a robe you will roll them up, like a garment they will be changed. But you are the same, and your years will have no end."

Isaiah 9:6. Hebrews 1:2. Colossians 1:17. Colossians 2:9. Hebrews 1:8, 10-12.

PRINCE OF PEACE.

Because of the tender mercy of our God . . . the sunrise shall visit us from on high to give light to those who sit in darkness and in the shadow of death, to guide our feet into the way of peace.

We have peace with God through our Lord Jesus Christ.

Jesus said . . . "Peace I leave with you; my peace I give to you. Not as the world gives do I give to you. Let not your hearts be troubled, neither let them be afraid."

"In the world you will have tribulation. But take heart; I have overcome the world."

For [Christ] himself is our peace.

Isaiah 9:6. Luke 1:78-79. Romans 5:1. John 14:9, 27. John 16:33. Ephesians 2:14.

[MARY] GAVE BIRTH TO HER FIRSTBORN SON AND WRAPPED HIM IN SWADDLING CLOTHS AND LAID HIM IN A MANGER, BECAUSE THERE WAS NO PLACE FOR THEM IN THE INN.

In the same region there were shepherds out in the field, keeping watch over their flock by night. And an angel of the Lord appeared to them. . . .

The angel said to them, "Fear not, for behold, I bring you good news of great joy that will be for all the people. For unto you is born this day in the city of David a Savior, who is Christ the Lord." . . . And suddenly there was with the angel a multitude of the heavenly host praising God.

The shepherds said to one another, "Let us go over to Bethlehem and see this thing that has happened, which the Lord has made known to us." And they went with haste and found Mary and Joseph, and the baby lying in a manger.

Luke 2:7-11, 13, 15-16.

THANKS BE TO GOD FOR HIS
INEXPRESSIBLE GIFT!

Make a joyful noise to the LORD, all the earth! Serve the LORD with gladness! Come into his presence with singing! Enter his gates with thanksgiving, and his courts with praise! Give thanks to him; bless his name!

Being found in human form, [Christ] humbled himself by becoming obedient to the point of death, even death on a cross. Therefore God has highly exalted him and bestowed on him the name that is above every name, so that at the name of Jesus every knee should bow, in heaven and on earth and under the earth, and every tongue confess that Jesus Christ is Lord, to the glory of God the Father.

2 Corinthians 9:15. Psalm 100:1-2, 4. Philippians 2:8-11.

GOD ANOINTED JESUS OF NAZARETH WITH THE
HOLY SPIRIT AND WITH POWER.

[Jesus] went about doing good and healing all who were oppressed by the devil, for God was with him.

And [Jesus] said to [Simon and Andrew], "Follow me, and I will make you fishers of men."

Bear one another's burdens, and so fulfill the law of Christ.

Do nothing from rivalry or conceit, but in humility count others more significant than yourselves.

Be kind to one another, tenderhearted, forgiving one another, as God in Christ forgave you.

Whoever says he abides in [Christ] ought to walk in the same way in which he walked.

Acts 10:38. Acts 10:38. Matthew 4:19. Galatians 6:2. Philippians 2:3.
Ephesians 4:32. 1 John 2:6.

NOW IS THE DAY OF SALVATION.

The old has passed away; behold, the new has come. All this is from God, who through Christ reconciled us to himself. . . . For our sake he made him to be sin who knew no sin, so that in him we might become the righteousness of God.

According to [God's] great mercy, he has caused us to be born again to a living hope through the resurrection of Jesus Christ from the dead, to an inheritance that is imperishable, undefiled, and unfading, kept in heaven for *us*.

Our citizenship is in heaven.

People will come from east and west, and from north and south, and recline at table in the kingdom of God.

The Lamb in the midst of the throne will be their shepherd, and he will guide them to springs of living water, and God will wipe away every tear from their eyes.

2 Corinthians 6:2. 2 Corinthians 5:17-18, 21. 1 Peter 1:3-4. Philippians 3:20.
Luke 13:29. Revelation 7:17.

AMEN. COME, LORD JESUS!

Behold, the Lord GOD comes with might, and his arm rules for him; behold, his reward is with him, and his recompense before him. He will tend his flock like a shepherd; he will gather the lambs in his arms.

We are waiting for new heavens and a new earth in which righteousness dwells. . . . Since you are waiting for these, be diligent to be found by him without spot or blemish, and at peace.

Now to him who is able to keep you from stumbling and to present you blameless before the presence of his glory with great joy . . . be glory, majesty, dominion, and authority, before all time and now and forever. Amen.

Revelation 22:20. Isaiah 40:10-11. 2 Peter 3:13-14. Jude 24-25.

PRAISE THE LORD!

Praise the LORD from the heavens; praise him in the heights! Praise him, all his angels; praise him, all his hosts! Praise him, sun and moon, praise him, all you shining stars! Praise him, you highest heavens, and you waters above the heavens! Let them praise the name of the LORD!

Praise the LORD from the earth, you great sea creatures and all deeps, fire and hail, snow and mist, stormy wind fulfilling his word! Mountains and all hills, fruit trees and all cedars! Beasts and all livestock, creeping things and flying birds!

Kings of the earth and all peoples, princes and all rulers of the earth! Young men and maidens together, old men and children! Let them praise the name of the LORD, for his name alone is exalted; his majesty is above earth and heaven.

Psalm 148:1 Psalm 148:1-5, 7-13.

KEEP YOURSELVES IN THE LOVE OF GOD.

Finally . . . whatever is true, whatever is honorable, whatever is just, whatever is pure, whatever is lovely, whatever is commendable, if there is any excellence, if there is anything worthy of praise, think about these things.

Continue in what you have learned and have firmly believed, knowing from whom you learned it.

The LORD is with you while you are with him. If you seek him, he will be found by you, but if you forsake him, he will forsake you.

Jude 21. Philippians 4:8. 2 Timothy 3:14. 2 Chronicles 15:2.

THE LORD SITS ENTHRONED FOREVER.

The LORD reigns; he is robed in majesty; the LORD is robed; he has put on strength as his belt. Yes, the world is established; it shall never be moved.

Yours, O LORD, is the greatness and the power and the glory and the victory and the majesty, for all that is in the heavens and in the earth is yours. Yours is the kingdom, O LORD, and you are exalted as head above all. Both riches and honor come from you, and you rule over all. In your hand are power and might, and in your hand it is to make great and to give strength to all. And now we thank you, our God, and praise your glorious name.

Your way, O God, is holy.

Psalm 9:7. Psalm 93:1. 1 Chronicles 29:11-13. Psalm 77:13.

> "Yours, O LORD, is the greatness and the power and the glory and the victory and the majesty."

Prayers, Notes, and Favorite Verses

Prayers, Notes, and Favorite Verses

Prayers, Notes, and Favorite Verses

Prayers, Notes, and Favorite Verses

Prayers, Notes, and Favorite Verses

Prayers, Notes, and Favorite Verses

Prayers, Notes, and Favorite Verses

Prayers, Notes, and Favorite Verses

Prayers, Notes, and Favorite Verses

Prayers, Notes, and Favorite Verses

Prayers, Notes, and Favorite Verses